NAKED CAKES

NAKED CAKES

simply stunning cakes

Hannah Miles

photography by Steve Painter

RYLAND PETERS & SMALL
LONDON • NEW YORK

*To my dear friends
Kathy and Simon Brown,
with love x*

**Design, photography and
prop styling** Steve Painter
Editor Kate Eddison
Production Gordana Simakovic
Art Director Leslie Harrington
Editorial Director Julia Charles
Publisher Cindy Richards

Food stylist Lucy McKelvie
Food stylist's assistant Scarlet
McKelvie
Indexer Hilary Bird

First published in 2015
This edition published in 2019
by Ryland Peters & Small
20–21 Jockey's Fields
London WC1R 4BW
and
341 E 116th St
New York NY 10029

www.rylandpeters.com

10 9 8 7 6 5 4 3 2 1

Text © Hannah Miles 2015, 2019
Design and photographs © Ryland
Peters & Small 2015, 2019

Printed in China

ISBN: 978-1-78879-119-9

A CIP record for this book is available
from the British Library.

US Library of Congress CIP data has
been applied for.

Disclaimer

The author has used food-safe,
pesticide-free flowers and edible petals
for decorative purposes in these
recipes. Flowers should be removed
before the cake is cut, and should
not be eaten. Neither the author nor
the publisher accept any liability for
harm or injury caused by consuming
flowers or parts of flowers.

Notes

• Use food-safe, pesticide-free flowers
and petals only for decorating cakes.
Flowers are for decoration only and
should be removed before cutting the
cake. Pollen is allergenic and should
not touch food. Only petals sold as
'edible' should be eaten. Never eat any
floral decoration unless you are certain
it is safe to do so.
• Both British (Metric) and American
(Imperial plus US cups) measurements
are included in these recipes for your
convenience, however it is important
to work with one set of measurements
and not alternate between the two.
• All spoon and cup measurements are
level unless otherwise specified.
• Eggs are medium (UK) or large (US),
unless otherwise specified. Uncooked
or partially cooked eggs should not be
served to the very old, frail, young
children, pregnant women or those
with compromised immune systems.
• When a recipe calls for the grated
zest of citrus fruit, buy unwaxed fruit
and wash well before using. If you can
only find treated fruit, scrub well in
warm soapy water before using.
• Ovens should be preheated to the
specified temperatures. We recommend
using an oven thermometer. If using a
fan-assisted oven, adjust temperatures
according to the manufacturer's
instructions.

contents

6 introduction

8 tips and techniques

11 using edible flowers

12 romantic charm

34 chic simplicity

58 vintage elegance

80 rustic style

100 dramatic effect

122 the changing seasons

142 index

144 acknowledgments

Introduction

For many years, celebration cakes for weddings and baptisms have been decorated with thick layers of icing and marzipan, birthday cakes have been covered in rich ganache toppings and sprinkles, and cupcakes have been swirled high with frosting. While there is definitely a place for such cakes, for me, all this decoration hides the natural beauty of the cake. In recent times there has been a resurgence of simple sponge cakes in place of traditional white iced wedding cakes, and these charming tiered sponge cakes are decorated with fresh flowers and fruits.

The concept of a 'naked cake' is a cake that is stripped bare. The decoration is kept as simple as possible, which lets the cake itself shine as the centrepiece. There are very few hard and fast rules with naked cakes, but the one essential requirement is that the sides of the sponges are on display and are not covered (although it is acceptable for them to have a small drizzle of icing, a dusting of icing/confectioners' sugar, or the thinnest layer of buttercream, provided that you can still see the sponge through the icing).

Decorations should be simple, but spectacular. One of my favourite ways to achieve this is by colouring the sponge layers in different colours, trimming away the cooked edges, so that the coloured cake itself is the decoration. Beautiful ombre effects can be achieved in this way. Baking a cake in a decoratively shaped pan, such as a Bundt pan, and then dusting with icing/confectioners' sugar to highlight the shapes can also be very pretty and overwhelmingly simple, particularly when the centre is filled with fresh berries. Or why not decorate a classic Victoria sponge cake with a pretty wreath of crystallized flowers picked from your own garden?

The cakes in this book are all perfect for special occasions when you need a stunning centrepiece. Most of the recipes are made using a basic sponge cake recipe (see page 9), with flavourings added.

The first chapter of this book, Romantic Charm, provides cakes that are suitable for celebrating the special person in your life and include a beautiful pink and pistachio layer cake (the cover of this book and my favourite recipe!) or the heart layer cake which makes a lovely natural wedding cake.

When it comes to beautiful cakes for everyday occasions, the Chic Simplicity chapter contains simple ideas such as mini clementine cakes, naked fondant fancies and a beautiful mint chocolate roulade decorated with frosted mint leaves.

In the Vintage Elegance chapter you will find an assortment of cakes that can take centre stage at any party table. The timbale cakes look so pretty stacked on a tall cake stand, dusted simply with icing/confectioners' sugar and topped with fresh flowers or why not try the macaron cake, inspired by the pâtisseries of Paris.

The Rustic Style chapter contains a beautiful charlotte royale with rings of Swiss roll/jelly roll encasing a delicious strawberry mousse. For pure simplicity, the Bundt cake has no decoration at all, other than a dusting of icing/confectioners' sugar to show off the shape of the pan or why not fill with fresh berries to add extra colour to the cake.

If you want to put on a bit more of a show, why not try one of the cakes from the Dramatic Effect chapter such as green tea ice cream cakes, decorated with cherry blossom branches or the spectacular coffee and pineapple cake. The chequerboard cake looks stunning with black and white squares, or why not try the peppermint and white chocolate cake with graded green layers?

Finally the Changing Seasons chapter contains cakes that are inspired by the year's seasons – lavender and lemon cakes for the summer, a delicious pumpkin cake in autumn and a simple Christmas cake with a crumble topping for winter.

No matter what the event, the recipes here will wow your guests and inspire them to enjoy the natural beauty of the humble sponge cake.

Tips and techniques

OMBRE EFFECT SPONGE LAYERS

Using gradating shades of one colour creates a very pretty pattern in naked cakes. Colour the layers of your sponge slightly different shades of the same colour so that when stacked, your cakes goes from a dark to a light shade.

When you have made the sponge cake batter for your recipe, add a few drops of food colouring to the batter and fold in. I use food colouring gels, as these give a stronger colour, but food colouring liquids also work just fine. Make sure that the food colouring is folded in completely.

If you are making a four-layer cake, once you have added the first colour, remove a quarter of the mixture from the mixing bowl. To do this, I level the cake mixture and then mark it into quarters on the top using a spatula and then carefully remove that portion of cake mixture and spoon it into one of the cake pans.

Next, add a few more drops of food colouring to the cake batter and fold in gently. This will turn the cake batter a slightly darker colour. You do not need to add a lot of food colouring to change the shade, as you only want the change to be gradual. Remove a third of the cake mixture and place in a separate cake pan.

Repeat by adding a few more drops of food colouring to the third and fourth portions of the cake mixture, and then bake your cakes following the recipe instructions.

When the cakes have cooked, turn them out onto a rack to cool. Once cooled completely, you need to trim away the sides of each cake carefully with a sharp knife to reveal the coloured sponge inside. It is important that the cakes are completely cold when you do this, otherwise the sponges can break. To cut away the edges, I place the cake flat on a board and cut down small slices of the cake with a sharp knife, turning the cake after each few cuts, so that you keep the circular shape of the cake.

DECORATING TIPS

The recipes in this book contain lots of ideas for naturally beautiful decorations, using edible flowers, sugar stencils and fresh fruit, but you can let your imagination run wild. When I am out shopping, I often find the perfect decoration that inspires a cake centrepiece, so you should keep your eyes open for ideas everywhere you go.

If you intend to use fresh petals as part of an edible decoration, it is important to make sure they are safe to consume (see page 11). Lots of flowers are safe to use with food, but, although edible, they taste quite bitter. Therefore, I recommend using food-safe flowers for decoration only and removing them before you cut the cake. Never eat floral decorations unless you are certain it is safe to do so.

If you do not have cake stencils, make your own by cutting out a cardboard template just larger than your cake and cutting out pretty patterns using a craft knife. To decorate the cake, simply place the stencil on top and dust with a thick layer of icing/confectioners' sugar or cocoa powder. You can even make interlocking double stencil designs and decorate with patterns in both icing/confectioners' sugar and cocoa, if you are feeling very creative. If you are short of time, simply use a doily instead.

One simple type of decoration is to tie cakes with ribbons and bows. These are available in haberdashers and good department stores, and come in a wide variety of patterns and colours. I usually secure the ribbon in place with a large dress-maker's pin, but it is essential that this is sterilized before using and is removed carefully before serving the cake.

VARYING THE CAKE QUANTITY

The recipes in this book generally make large celebration cakes that will serve 12–14 people, but if you have a smaller or larger gathering it is possible to scale the cakes up or down.

To reduce a three-tiered cake to a two-tiered cake, reduce the cake batter by one-third and cook in two cake pans rather than three.

If you want to make a larger cake with more tiers, you can increase the cake batter mixture and then use more cake pans to create additional layers. If you want to make a three-tier round sponge cake with four layers, simply increase the recipe quantity by one-third and use a fourth cake pan. The actual quantity of additional cake mixture you need will depend on the size of cake pans you are using, so it isn't possible to give exact conversions.

LAYERING CAKES

The cakes in this book are easy to layer as they are not very large and no additional equipment is needed. To stack cakes, simply place the largest cake in the centre of your cake stand or serving plate. Decorate following the instructions in the recipe and then place the next cake on top. It is important that you place the cake directly in the centre so that the stack is balanced. If there is a third layer in the recipe, place the smallest cake on top in the same way.

If you are making a large cake, such as a wedding cake, it will be necessary to assemble the cakes slightly differently to ensure that they do not collapse. Place each cake on a lightweight cake board that is the same size (or very slightly larger) than each cake layer. Place the largest cake on your serving board and then slide several short doweling rods into the cake to support the next tier. The rods must be the same height as your cake, so that they do not stick out – measure carefully and cut them to size. Once the rods are inserted, place the next cake and board on top and repeat until your cake is fully tiered. I advise you to transport the individual cakes to your venue and assemble once you are there to ensure stable results. Cake boards and dowels are available in baking stores and online.

Basic sponge cake mixture

These basic recipes are used in most of the recipes in this book. Simply select the quantity of cake batter called for by your recipe and prepare as follows.

Use an electric whisk to mix the butter and sugar in a bowl until light and creamy. Add the eggs and whisk again. Fold in the flour, baking powder and buttermilk or sour cream using a spatula, until incorporated. Use as directed in your recipe.

2-egg Cake Batter

115 g/1 stick butter, softened

115 g/generous ½ cup caster/granulated sugar

2 eggs

115 g/generous ¾ cup self-raising/self-rising flour, sifted

1 teaspoon baking powder

1 tablespoon buttermilk or sour cream

4-egg Cake Batter

225 g/2 sticks butter, softened

225 g/generous 1 cup caster/granulated sugar

4 eggs

225 g/1¼ cups self-raising/self-rising flour, sifted

2 teaspoons baking powder

2 tablespoons buttermilk or sour cream

5-egg Cake Batter

280 g/2½ sticks butter, softened

280 g/1½ cups caster/granulated sugar

5 eggs

280 g/generous 2 cups self-raising/self-rising flour, sifted

2½ teaspoons baking powder

2½ tablespoons buttermilk or sour cream

6-egg Cake Batter

340 g/3 sticks butter, softened

340 g/1¾ cups caster/granulated sugar

6 eggs

340 g/2½ cups self-raising/self-rising flour, sifted

3 teaspoons baking powder

3 tablespoons buttermilk or sour cream

Using edible flowers

Flowers have been used in cooking for centuries and they are a perfect decoration for naked cakes because of their natural beauty. So many flowers are edible and they can be used in both fresh and crystallized form. Some flowers are poisonous, so you must never eat a floral decoration unless you are certain it is safe to do so. They must also not have been sprayed with chemicals or pesticides, as these are harmful.

LIST OF EDIBLE FLOWERS

The following list was compiled by my wonderful friend and edible flower expert, Kathy Brown, to whom I am forever grateful for introducing me to her edible flower garden and sharing her knowledge and love of flowers with me. Never eat any floral decorations unless you are certain it is safe to do so.

Hollyhocks (Alcea rosea)

Lemon Verbena flowers and leaves (Aloysia triphylla)

Anchusa (Anchusa azurea)

Dill flowers (Anethum graveolens)

Daisy (Bellis perennis)

Borage (Borago officinalis)

Pot marigolds (Calendula officinalis)

Camomile (Chamaemelum nobile)

Citrus flowers (Citrus sinensis and citrus limon)

Saffron (Crocus sativus)

Courgette flowers (Cucurbita pepo var courgette or marrow)

Alpine pinks (Dianthus)

Salad rocket flowers (Eruca vescaria ssp. sativa)

Fennel flowers (Foeniculum vulgare)

Sweet woodruff (Galium odoratum)

Sunflower petals (Helianthus annuus)

Day lily (Hemerocallis)

Sweet rocket (Hesperis matronalis)

Hibiscus (Hibiscus rosa-sinensis)

Hops (Humulus lupulus)

Hyssop (Hyssopsus officinalis)

Lavender (Lavendula angustifolia)

Tiger lily (Lilium lancifolium)

Apple mint (Menthe suaveolens)

Bergamot (Monarda didyma)

Sweet cicely (Myrrhis odorata)

Basil flowers (Ocimum basilicum)

Nasturtium (Tropaeolum majus)

Evening primrose (Oenothera biennis)

Wild marjoram/oregano (Origanum vulgare)

Scented geraniums (Pelargonium)

Cowslip (Primula veris)

Primrose (Primula vulgaris)

Rose (Rosa)

Rosemary (Rosmarimus officinalis)

Sage flowers (Salvia officinalis)

Dandelion (Taraxacum officinale)

Thyme (Thymus vulgaris)

Clover flowers (Trifolium pratense)

Sweet violet (Viola odorata)

Viola (Viola)

Lemon balm (Melissa officinalis aurea)

CRYSTALLIZING FLOWERS

To crystallize edible petals, flowers or leaves, you will need 1 egg white and some caster/superfine sugar. Make sure that the petals, flowers and leaves are unblemished and clean. Whisk the egg white until very foamy using a whisk, then paint the egg white on both the front and the back of the petals, flowers or leaves using a small, clean paint brush and sprinkle with caster/superfine sugar. This is best done by holding the sugar at a small height above the petal, flower or leaf and sprinkling. Repeat with all the petals, flowers or leaves, one at a time, and place on a silicon mat or sheet of baking parchment on a baking sheet. Leave in a warm place to dry overnight. Once dried, stored the petals, flowers or leaves in an airtight container, layered gently in baking parchment. They will keep for 1–2 months.

Romantic Charm

Pistachio layer cake

One of the prettiest decorations for a naked cake can be achieved by adding food colouring to your cake batter. By dividing the cake batter between several bowls and colouring each with different quantities of food colouring, you can achieve gradating coloured tiered cakes that look stunning on any party table. This is my version, from vibrant to pale pink, with a pale green pistachio filling. If you prefer cakes without nuts, simply layer the cakes with fresh cream and jam instead.

3 teaspoons pure vanilla extract

1 recipe 6-egg Cake Batter (see page 9)

pink food colouring gel

FOR THE PISTACHIO CREAM

200 g/1⅓ cups shelled pistachio nuts

2 heaped tablespoons icing/confectioners' sugar

600 ml/2⅓ cups double/heavy cream

5 x 20-cm/8-inch round cake pans, greased and lined with baking parchment

a piping/pastry bag fitted with round nozzle/tip

Serves 12

To prepare the pistachio cream, blitz three-quarters of the pistachios in a food processor with the icing/confectioners' sugar to very fine crumbs. Set aside until you are ready to assemble the cake. Coarsely chop the remaining pistachios, and set aside for the decoration.

Preheat the oven to 180°C (350°F) Gas 4.

Fold the vanilla extract into the cake batter and divide the mixture equally between 5 bowls. Add a little food colouring to each, adding a very small amount in the first bowl and then increasing gradually in each bowl so that you have gradating colours of cake batter. Spoon each batter into a prepared cake pan. (If you do not have 5 pans, then cook the cakes in batches, washing, greasing and re-lining the cake pans between cooking.) Bake for 20–25 minutes, until the cakes spring back to the touch and a knife inserted into the centre of each cake comes out clean. Leave to cool in the pans for a few minutes, then turn out onto a wire rack to cool completely.

If the sides of the cakes have browned slightly during cooking, once cool, use a sharp knife to trim the sides of the cake carefully to expose the pink colour.

Put the double/heavy cream in a large bowl with the ground pistachio and icing/confectioners' sugar mixture, and whisk to stiff peaks with an electric mixer or whisk. Spoon the cream into the piping/pastry bag.

Place the darkest pink cake on a serving plate and pipe a thick swirl of cream on top, ensuring that the cream goes to the edge of the cake. Repeat with the remaining cakes, stacking them in colour order from darkest to lightest. Once the final layer is in place, smooth the edges of the cream using a palette knife or metal spatula. Pipe a layer of cream on top and smooth it neatly using a palette knife or metal spatula, then gently press the chopped pistachios around the edge of the cream.

Serve straight away or store in the refrigerator until you are ready to serve. As the cake contains fresh cream, it is best eaten on the day it is made, although it will keep for up to 2 days in the refrigerator.

Valentine's layer cake

This cake makes a perfect celebration centrepiece for a wedding or special anniversary, with three tiered hearts decorated with fresh roses. Heart-shaped pans are available from good cook shops and online, and are also available to hire. If you do not have heart-shaped pans, you can make this cake by cutting out hearts from three square cakes – use the sizes below as a guide to draw hearts on a piece of cardboard, then cut them out and use them as templates to cut out the cake hearts with a sharp knife. If you want to make a smaller version of this cake with two tiers, just use half of the cake batter and the two smaller heart-shaped pans.

2 teaspoons pure vanilla extract

double recipe 4-egg Cake Batter (see page 9)

food-safe, pesticide-free pink flowers, such as roses

FOR THE FROSTING

100 g/scant 1 cup cream cheese

500 g/3½ cups icing/ confectioners' sugar, sifted

50 g/3½ tablespoons butter, softened

a little milk (if needed)

16-cm/6½-inch, 20-cm/8-inch and 26-cm/10½-inch heart-shaped cake pans, greased and lined with baking parchment

Serves 20

Preheat the oven to 180°C (350°F) Gas 4.

Fold the vanilla extract into the cake batter and divide the mixture between the prepared cake pans, adding less to the smaller cake pan and more to the larger one, so the batter is of equal depth in all.

Bake the cakes for about 40–55 minutes, until the cakes spring back to the touch and a knife inserted into the centre of each cake comes out clean. The smaller cakes will take less time to cook than the larger one, so check them regularly towards the end of the cooking time. Leave to cool in the pans for a few minutes, then turn out onto a wire rack to cool completely.

For the frosting, whisk together the cream cheese, icing/ confectioners' sugar and butter until you have a smooth, thick frosting, adding a little milk if it is too stiff.

Cut each cake in half with a large, serrated knife, then sandwich each one back together with a thin layer of frosting. Place the largest heart cake on your serving board and completely cover with a layer of frosting, scraping the frosting very thinly on the sides of the cake so that you can see the cake through the frosting. Top with the middle-sized heart and repeat the above steps, then do the same with the smallest cake so that you have a stack of hearts, all covered in a thin layer of buttercream. Leave the frosting to set, and then decorate with roses around each layer of the cake.

If you use whole flowers to decorate, these will not be edible (the stems and inner part of the flower are very bitter), so they are for decorative purposes only and should be removed as you cut the cake. Never eat floral decorations unless you are certain is it safe to do so.

This cake will keep for up to 2 days stored in an airtight container, although it is best eaten on the day it is made.

Strawberry layer cake with Chantilly cream

This is a perfect summertime cake with cream and fresh berries and perfectly scented with vanilla. If you want to make a smaller cake, you can use a 4-egg cake batter and make the cake in the smaller 20-cm/8-inch square pan instead, halving the quantity of cream and strawberries. If possible, use real vanilla seeds in the Chantilly cream rather than vanilla extract, as it gives a better flavour. If you are lucky enough to find wild strawberries, these make beautiful decorations.

1 teaspoon vanilla bean powder or 2 teaspoons pure vanilla extract

1 recipe 6-egg Cake Batter (see page 9)

600 g/21 oz. strawberries

5 tablespoons strawberry jam/jelly

icing/confectioners' sugar, for dusting

a few strawberry leaves, for decoration

FOR THE CHANTILLY CREAM

600 ml/2½ cups double/ heavy cream

1 teaspoon vanilla bean powder or seeds of one vanilla pod/bean

2 tablespoons icing/ confectioners' sugar, sifted

20-cm/8-inch and 25-cm/10-inch square loose-bottomed cake pans, greased and lined with baking parchment

Serves 18

Preheat the oven to 180°C (350°F) Gas 4.

Fold the vanilla into the cake batter and spoon the mixture into the prepared cake pans, dividing the mixture approximately two-thirds into the larger pan and the remaining one-third into the smaller pan, so that the depth of the cakes is equal. Bake in the preheated oven for 30–40 minutes, until the cakes are golden brown and spring back to the touch and a knife inserted into the centre of each cake comes out clean. The smaller cake will take less time to cook than the larger one, so check it regularly towards the end of the cooking time. Leave the cakes to cool in the pans for a few minutes, then turn out onto a wire rack to cool completely.

For the Chantilly cream, put the cream, vanilla and icing/ confectioners' sugar in a large bowl and whisk to stiff peaks.

Set aside one or two of the whole strawberries for decoration, then hull and slice the remaining fruit.

Cut each cake in half horizontally using a large serrated knife. Place the bottom half of the larger cake on a serving plate and spread cream across the surface. Cover the cream with some of the strawberry slices and 3 tablespoons of the jam. Top with the second large cake half and dust the top with icing/confectioners' sugar. Spoon a tablespoonful of the jam in the centre and spread out a little, keeping it in the centre of the cake so that it will all be covered by the smaller cake – this will hold the smaller cake in place. Place the bottom of the smaller cake on top of the jam and repeat the above steps with the cream and the remaining strawberries and jam. Place the second half of the small cake on top and dust with icing/confectioners' sugar. Decorate with the reserved whole strawberries and a few strawberry leaves. The leaves should be removed before you cut the cake.

Serve straight away or store in the refrigerator until you are ready to serve. As the cake contains fresh cream, it is best eaten on the day it is made.

Turkish delight cake

This charming cake with pink and yellow layers is topped with glistening Turkish delight and looks as pretty as a picture. It is scented with rose to mirror the flavour of the Turkish delight, and is filled with rose petal cream and rose jam. If you find the flavour of rose overpowering, simply replace with unflavoured whipped cream and raspberry jam for equally delicious results.

1 tablespoon rose syrup
or rosewater

1 recipe 4-egg Cake Batter
(see page 9)

pink food colouring

3 tablespoons rose jam
(or raspberry jam)

icing/confectioners' sugar,
for dusting

pink and yellow Turkish
delight, cut into small pieces

FOR THE ROSE CREAM

a handful of edible, pesticide-
free, scented rose petals

1 tablespoon rose syrup

1 tablespoon icing/
confectioners' sugar, sifted

1 tablespoon flavourless oil,
such as vegetable or sunflower
oil

400 ml/1¾ cups double/
heavy cream

*2 x 20-cm/8-inch round cake
pans, greased and lined with
baking parchment*

Serves 10

Preheat the oven to 180°C (350°F) Gas 4.

Fold the rose syrup into the cake batter using a spatula and spoon half of the mixture into one of the prepared cake pans. Add a few drops of pink food colouring to the remaining batter and whisk in to obtain an even colour. Spoon the pink cake batter into the second pan. Bake for 25–30 minutes, until the cakes spring back to the touch and a knife inserted into the centre of each cake comes out clean. Leave the cakes to cool in the pans for a few minutes, then turn out onto a wire rack to cool completely.

For the rose cream, blitz the rose petals, rose syrup, icing/confectioners' sugar and oil to a paste in a food processor. Put the rose paste in a mixing bowl with the cream, and whisk to stiff peaks.

Using a large, serrated knife, trim away the edges of the cake to reveal the pink and yellow sponge inside. Cut each cake in half horizontally. Place one of the pink cake halves on your serving plate and spread one-third of the rose cream over the surface. Top with a little jam and spread out gently, then place one of the yellow cake halves on top. Repeat the cream and jam steps until all four cake halves are layered in alternating colours. Smooth the edges of the cream using a palette knife or metal spatula.

Dust the top of the cake with some icing/confectioners' sugar, then decorate the top of the cake with the Turkish delight.

Serve straight away or store in the refrigerator until you are ready to serve. As the cake contains fresh cream, it is best eaten on the day it is made, but it can be stored in the refrigerator for up to 2 days.

Miniature wedding cakes

I love these miniature wedding cakes – they are so pretty and you can let your creativity run wild with the decoration. You could even serve them in place of a main cake at a wedding, giving each guest an individual cake. The cakes are covered in a very thin layer of fondant icing, which seals the cake and means that they will keep well for several days. You can flavour the cakes in any way you choose. These are simple sponge, but you can add citrus zest, chocolate chips or a little apple purée if you wish. The possibilities are endless!

1 recipe 5-egg Cake Batter (see page 9)

400 g/2¾ cups fondant icing/confectioners' sugar, sifted

food-safe flowers, such as pesticide-free roses, or sugar flowers, to decorate

FOR THE ICING

250 g/1¾ cups icing/confectioners' sugar, sifted

10 g/½ tablespoon butter, softened

1 tablespoon cream cheese

½ teaspoon vanilla bean powder or 1 teaspoon pure vanilla extract

a little milk (if needed)

a 40 x 28-cm/16 x 11-inch shallow rectangular baking pan, greased and lined with baking parchment

9-cm/3½-inch, 6½-cm/2½-inch and 4-cm/1½-inch round cutters

Makes 6

Preheat the oven to 180°C (350°F) Gas 4.

Spoon the cake batter into the prepared baking pan and bake in the preheated oven for 30–40 minutes, until the cake is golden brown and springs back to the touch and a knife comes out clean when inserted into the centre of the cake. Leave to cool in the pan for a few minutes, then turn out onto a wire rack to cool completely.

For the buttercream, whisk together the icing/confectioners' sugar, butter, cream cheese and vanilla until you have a smooth, stiff icing, adding a little milk if the mixture is too stiff.

Using the cutters, cut out 6 circles of cake with each cutter. Spread a little buttercream on the base of each of the middle-sized circles and place one on top of each larger circle. Repeat with the small circles, fixing one on top of each cake stack with a little buttercream, so that you have 6 miniature wedding cakes.

For the icing, heat the fondant icing/confectioners' sugar with 80–100 ml/about ⅓ cup water until you have a smooth, runny and almost translucent icing. Place the 6 cakes on a wire rack with a sheet of foil or baking parchment underneath to catch any icing drips. Using a spoon, drizzle the cakes with a thin layer of icing so that they are completely covered. If you are using sugar flowers, you should add them at this stage before the icing sets. Otherwise, leave the icing to set. Slide a sharp knife under each cake to release them from the rack.

Decorate each cake with fresh flowers when you are ready to serve. If you use whole flowers to decorate, these will not be edible (the stems and inner part of the flower are very bitter), so they are for decorative purposes only and should be removed as you cut the cake. Never eat floral decorations unless you are certain they are safe to consume.

These cakes will keep for up to 3 days stored in an airtight container.

Peach melba meringue layer

The famous singer Dame Nellie Melba loved the retro dessert peach melba – ice cream and peaches – which is the inspiration for this decadent layer cake. With crisp meringue, poached peaches, raspberries and cream, this cake is ideal for special occasions. If you want to make a smaller cake, simply halve the meringue and cake quantities and just have one cake layer and one meringue.

1 teaspoon vanilla bean paste or pure vanilla extract

1 recipe 4-egg Cake Batter (see page 9)

icing/confectioners' sugar, for dusting

FOR THE MERINGUE

4 egg whites

225g/1 cup plus 1 tablespoon caster/superfine sugar

FOR THE PEACH FILLING

8 peaches

500 ml/2 cups double/heavy cream, whipped

400 g/14 oz. raspberries

2 x 20-cm/8-inch round cake pans, greased and lined with baking parchment

2 baking sheets, lined with baking parchment

Serves 12

Preheat the oven to 140°C (275°F) Gas 1.

To prepare the meringue, whisk the egg whites to stiff peaks using an electric hand mixer. Add the sugar, a spoonful at a time, whisking after each spoonful until you have a thick glossy meringue that holds a peak when you lift the beaters.

On the prepared baking sheets, make two 20-cm/8-inch circles of meringue, swirling the tops into decorative peaks. Bake in the preheated oven for 1½ hours, until the meringues are crisp, then leave to cool on the baking sheet. Turn the oven up to 180°C (350°F) Gas 4.

Fold the vanilla into the cake batter and divide the mixture equally between the prepared cake pans. Bake for 20–30 minutes, until the cakes are golden brown and spring back to the touch and a knife inserted into the centre of each cake comes out clean. Leave to cool in the pans for a few minutes, then turn out onto a wire rack to cool completely.

Put the peaches in a bowl and pour over boiling water to cover them. Leave for a few minutes, then drain. When the peaches are just cool enough to handle, peel away their skins, which will have been loosened by the hot water. Remove the stones/pits and cut the flesh into slices.

To assemble, place one of the cakes on a serving plate and dust with icing/confectioners' sugar. Top with one-third of the whipped cream and cover with half of the peach slices. Place one of the meringues on top and cover that with one-third of the cream and the raspberries. Next place the second sponge on top and dust with icing/confectioners' sugar. Cover with the remaining cream and peaches. To finish, place the second meringue on top and dust with a little more icing/confectioners' sugar.

Serve straight away or store in the refrigerator until you are ready to serve. As the cake contains fresh cream, it is best eaten on the day it is made, although it will keep for up to 2 days in the refrigerator.

Rose petal cake

Using roses in baking is one of the things I love to do – their delicate fragrance reminds me of warm summer days when the scent of roses fills the air in my garden. This is a large cake, perfect for a celebration tea.

2 teaspoons vanilla extract

1 recipe 6-egg Cake Batter (see page 9)

edible dried rose petals, to decorate

FOR THE PETALS

pesticide-free, edible rose petals

1 egg white

1 teaspoon rosewater

caster/superfine sugar, for sprinkling

FOR THE FILLING

a handful of pesticide-free, edible rose petals

1 tablespoon rose syrup

1 tablespoon icing/confectioners' sugar

400 ml/1¾ cups double/heavy cream

rose petal jam

a paint brush

a baking sheet, lined with a silicone mat or baking parchment

3 x 20-cm/8-inch round cake pans, greased and lined with baking parchment

a piping/pastry bag fitted with a large star nozzle/tip

Serves 10

Begin by preparing the crystallized rose petals, as they need to dry overnight. Whisk together the egg white and rosewater until very foamy. Using a paint brush, paint the egg white on both the front and the back of the petals and sprinkle with sugar. This is best done by holding the sugar just above the flower and sprinkling. Have a plate below to catch the excess sugar. Repeat with all the petals, covering them one at a time, and place on the prepared baking sheet. Leave in a warm place to dry overnight. Once dried, stored the petals in an airtight container until you are ready to serve.

Preheat the oven to 180°C (350°F) Gas 4.

Fold the vanilla into the cake batter and divide the mixture equally between the prepared cake pans. Bake for 20–30 minutes, until the cakes are golden brown and spring back to the touch and a knife inserted into the centre of each cake comes out clean. Let cool in the pans for a few minutes, then turn out onto a wire rack to cool completely.

For the filling, put the rose petals in a food processor with the rose syrup and icing/confectioners' sugar and blitz to a smooth paste. Put the rose petal paste and cream in a large bowl and whisk to stiff peaks using a mixer. Transfer to a piping/pastry bag fitted with a star nozzle/tip.

Place one of the cakes on a serving plate and pipe one-third of the rose cream on top. Spoon over some of the rose petal jam. Place a second cake on top and cover with half of the remaining cream and more rose petal jam. Place the final cake on top. Spread the rest of the rose cream on top using a palette knife or metal spatula, then decorate with the crystallized rose petals in the middle and a ring of edible dried rose petals around the edge.

Serve straight away or store in the refrigerator until you are ready to serve. As the cake contains fresh cream, it is best eaten on the day it is made, although it will keep for up to 2 days in the refrigerator.

Neapolitan cakes

These pretty layer cakes are inspired by the classic pink, white and brown layered Neapolitan ice cream. With a rich chocolate layer, a simple vanilla layer, and a pretty strawberry sponge layer, these cakes can be assembled in any order you like.

1 recipe 6-egg Cake Batter (see page 9)

100 g/3½ oz. plain/bittersweet chocolate, melted

1 teaspoon vanilla extract

pink food colouring gel

FOR THE FILLING

500 g/3½ cups icing/confectioners' sugar, sifted

30 g/2 tablespoons butter, softened

½ teaspoon vanilla bean powder or 1 teaspoon pure vanilla extract

a little milk (if needed)

a few drops of pink food colouring gel

2 tablespoons unsweetened cocoa powder, sifted

TO DECORATE

2 tablespoons chocolate curls

2 tablespoons crushed honeycomb

2 tablespoons freeze-dried raspberry or strawberry pieces

3 x 20-cm/8-inch square cake pans, greased and lined with baking parchment

4-cm/1½-inch round pastry/cookie cutter

Makes 16

Preheat the oven to 180°C (350°F) Gas 4.

Divide the cake batter equally between 3 bowls. Add the melted chocolate to one bowl. Fold in gently, then spoon into one of the prepared cake pans. Add the vanilla to the second bowl and fold in. Spoon into another prepared cake pan. Finally, fold a few drops of pink food colouring gel into the third bowl and spoon the mixture into the last cake pan.

Bake the cakes in the preheated oven for 20–25 minutes, until firm to the touch and a knife inserted into the centre of each cake comes out clean. Let cool in the pans for a few minutes, then turn out onto a wire rack to cool completely.

For the buttercream filling, whisk together the icing/confectioners' sugar, butter and vanilla until you have a smooth, stiff icing, adding a little milk if the mixture is too stiff. Divide the buttercream into 3 bowls. Add a little pink food colouring gel to one portion and the sifted cocoa powder to another portion; leave the third portion plain.

To assemble, use the cutter to cut out 16 rounds of each cake. Assemble 3 different coloured discs of cake in any order you like, sandwiched together with the different buttercreams, spreading it on with a palette knife or metal spatula.

Finish the cakes off with a sprinkle of decoration: chocolate curls on the chocolate tops, crushed honeycomb on the white tops and freeze-dried raspberry or strawberry pieces on the pink tops.

These cakes will keep for up to 2 days stored in an airtight container, although they are best eaten on the day they are made.

Red velvet cake

Red velvet cake is an American favourite, flavoured with cocoa and chocolate and coloured with red food colouring. This cake is coated in a thin layer of buttercream and white roses, and would make a stunning wedding cake.

60 g/scant ⅔ cup unsweetened cocoa powder

1 recipe 6-egg Cake Batter (see page 9)

100 g/3½ oz. plain/bittersweet chocolate, melted

red food colouring gel

food-safe, pesticide-free white roses, to decorate

FOR THE FROSTING

200 g/scant 1 cup cream cheese

400 g/2¾ cups icing/ confectioners' sugar, sifted

50 g/3½ tablespoons butter, softened

a little milk (if needed)

3 x 20-cm/8-inch round cake pans, greased and lined with baking parchment

2 x 12-cm/5-inch round springform cake pans, greased and lined with baking parchment

Serves 14

Preheat the oven to 180°C (350°F) Gas 4.

Sift the cocoa powder into the cake batter and, using a spatula, fold in, together with the melted chocolate and a few drops of red food colouring. Divide the mixture between the prepared cake pans, adding less to the smaller cake pans and more to the larger ones so the batter is of equal depth in all. Bake for about 20–25 minutes, until the cakes spring bake to the touch and a knife inserted into the centre of each cake comes out clean. The smaller cakes will take less time to cook than the larger ones, so check regularly towards the end of the cooking time. Leave to cool in the pans for a few minutes, then turn out onto a wire rack to cool completely.

For the frosting, whisk together the cream cheese, icing/ confectioners' sugar and butter until you have a smooth, stiff icing, adding a little milk if the frosting is too stiff.

Place one of the larger cakes on a serving plate and cover with a layer of buttercream. Top with the next large cake and repeat the steps so that you have a stack of the three larger cakes. Spread a little icing in the centre of the stack of cakes and place one of the smaller cakes on top. Spread the top of the smaller cake with a little of the frosting, then place the final cake on top. Using a round-bladed knife, spread the thinnest layer possible of frosting over the cake so that the cake is still visible through the frosting. Decorate with the roses. If you use whole flowers to decorate, these will not be edible (the stems and inner part of the flower are very bitter), so they are for decorative purposes only and should be removed as you cut the cake. Do not eat any floral decorations unless you are certain it is safe to do so.

This cake will keep for up to 2 days stored in an airtight container, although it is best eaten on the day it is made.

Blueberry and lemon drizzle cakes

Tangy blueberries and zesty lemon are the perfect combination in these little cakes. Filled with whipped cream and lemon curd, these are great to serve for a tea party, topped with a few juicy blueberries.

grated zest of 2 lemons

1 recipe 4-egg Cake Batter (see page 9)

200 ml/¾ cup double/heavy cream, whipped

4 tablespoons lemon curd

200 g/1½ cups blueberries

FOR THE ICING

170 g/1¼ cups fondant icing/confectioners' sugar, sifted

freshly squeezed juice of 2 lemons

8 x 6.5-cm/2½-inch cake rings, greased and placed on a greased baking sheet

a piping/pastry bag fitted with large round nozzle/tip (optional)

a piping/pastry bag fitted with star nozzle/tip

Makes 8

Preheat the oven to 180°C (350°F) Gas 4.

Fold the lemon zest into the cake batter and divide the mixture equally between the prepared cake rings. You can do this either by spooning the batter in, or by putting the batter in a piping/pastry bag and piping it in neatly.

Bake in the preheated oven for 20–30 minutes, until the cakes are golden brown and spring back to the touch. Leave the cakes to cool in the rings for a few minutes, then remove by sliding a sharp knife around the inside of each ring. Transfer the cakes to a wire rack and leave to cool completely.

Cut each cake in half and pipe a swirl of the whipped cream onto each bottom cake half using the piping/pastry bag with the star nozzle/tip. Top with a little lemon curd and a few blueberries, then place the top cake half on.

For the icing, mix together the fondant icing/confectioners' sugar and lemon juice (add the lemon juice gradually as you may not need it all), until you have a smooth, thick icing. Spoon the icing over the tops of the cakes, drizzling a few drops over the sides, and leave to set for a few minutes. Decorate with a few blueberries and leave the icing to set.

Store in the refrigerator until you are ready to serve. As these cakes contain fresh cream, they are best eaten on the day they are made, although they will keep for up to 2 days in the refrigerator, if necessary.

Chic Simplicity

Lemon and raspberry roulade

Roulades are beautifully light and airy cakes, and make great dinner party desserts. Topped with just a dusting of powdered sugar and some white chocolate-dipped raspberries, this fresh and fruity cake is simply elegant and tastes delicious.

150 ml/⅔ cup milk

40 g/generous ¼ cup self-raising/self-rising flour, sifted

5 eggs, separated

150 g/¾ cup caster/granulated sugar

grated zest of 2 lemons

icing/confectioners' sugar, for dusting

FOR THE FILLING

400 ml/1¾ cups double/heavy cream

4 tablespoons ready-made custard/custard sauce

400 g/14 oz. (about 3½ cups) raspberries

FOR THE DECORATION

50 g/2 oz. white chocolate, melted

a 38 x 28-cm/15 x 11-inch Swiss roll/jelly roll pan, greased and lined with baking parchment

a baking sheet, lined with a silicone mat or baking parchment paper

Serves 6–8

Preheat the oven to 200°C (400°F) Gas 6.

Heat the milk and flour together in a saucepan over low heat and whisk to a smooth paste.

In a mixing bowl, whisk the egg yolks and sugar together until thick and creamy and voluminous. Beat in the flour mixture and the grated lemon zest.

In a separate mixing bowl, whisk the egg whites to stiff peaks. Adding one-third at a time, fold the egg whites into the cake batter. Pour the mixture into the prepared pan and spread out evenly. Take care to handle the mixture gently so that you do not knock all the air out of it. Bake in the preheated oven for 8–12 minutes, until the sponge springs back to the touch and is golden brown.

Lay a sheet of non-stick baking parchment, larger than the size of the pan, on a flat surface. Dust with icing/confectioners' sugar. Remove the roulade from the oven and turn out onto the dusted parchment. Remove the lining paper, then roll the sponge up using the dusted parchment, so that the paper is inside the roll, and let cool.

When you are ready to serve, whip the cream to stiff peaks. Unroll the roulade. Using a spatula, spread a layer of whipped cream, followed by a layer of custard, onto the sponge. Sprinkle most of the raspberries evenly on top, reserving about 10 for decoration. Roll up the roulade, place it on a serving plate and dust with a little extra icing/confectioners' sugar.

Place the melted white chocolate in a small bowl and dip the reserved raspberries in to half-coat in the chocolate. Drizzle a little of the melted white chocolate along the top of the roulade to help the raspberries stick, then arrange the raspberries on the top. Serve straight away.

Clementine cakes

I love the delicate citrus flavour of clementines. Decorated with a light touch of clementine icing and pretty rose petals, these mini cakes are perfect for afternoon tea.

1 recipe 2-egg Cake Batter (see page 9)

1 tablespoon clementine juice

grated zest of 2 clementines, plus extra to decorate

FOR THE ICING

170 g/1¼ cups fondant icing/confectioners' sugar, sifted

40 ml/3 tablespoons clementine juice

FOR THE PETALS

20–30 edible, pesticide-free orange rose petals

1 egg white

caster/superfine sugar, for dusting

a paint brush

a baking sheet, lined with a silicone mat or baking parchment

10 x 8-cm/3-inch cake rings, greased and placed on a greased baking sheet

a piping/pastry bag fitted with large round nozzle/tip (optional)

Makes 10

Begin by preparing the crystallized rose petals, as they need to dry overnight. Whisk the egg white until very foamy. Using a paint brush, paint the egg white on both the front and the back of the petals and sprinkle with sugar. This is best done by holding the sugar just above the petal and sprinkling. Have a plate below to catch the excess sugar. Repeat with all the petals, covering them one at a time, and place on the prepared baking sheet. Leave in a warm place to dry overnight. Once dried, stored the petals in an airtight container until you are ready to serve.

Preheat the oven to 180°C (350°F) Gas 4.

Fold the clementine juice and zest into the cake batter and divide the mixture equally between the prepared cake rings. You can do this either by spooning the batter in, or by putting the batter in a piping/pastry bag and piping it in neatly. Bake in the preheated oven for 20–30 minutes, until the cakes are golden brown and spring back to the touch and a knife inserted into the centre of each cake comes out clean. Leave the cakes to cool in the rings for a few minutes, then remove by sliding a sharp knife around the inside of each ring. Transfer the cakes to a wire rack and leave to cool completely.

For the icing, mix the fondant icing/confectioners' sugar with the clementine juice until it is just runny, and spoon a little over the top of each cake. Decorate with the crystallized rose petals and some grated clementine zest, and leave until the icing is set.

These cakes are best eaten on the day they are made, but will store for up to 2 days in an airtight container.

Lemon meringue cake

This cake is inspired by the popular dessert lemon meringue pie, with gradated yellow lemon drizzle cake slices, filled with buttercream and lemon curd, and topped with a billowing Italian meringue topping.

grated zest of 3 lemons

1 recipe 6-egg Cake Batter (see page 9)

yellow food colouring gel

FOR THE DRIZZLE

freshly squeezed juice of 3 lemons

3 tablespoons icing/confectioners' sugar

2 tablespoons lemon curd

FOR THE FILLING

350 g/2½ cups icing/confectioners' sugar, sifted

2 tablespoons butter, softened

1–2 tablespoons milk (if needed)

FOR THE MERINGUE TOPPING

100 g/½ cup caster/superfine sugar

1 tablespoon golden syrup/light corn syrup

2 egg whites

3 x 20-cm/8-inch round cake pans, greased and lined with baking parchment

a piping/pastry bag fitted with large star nozzle/tip

a chef's blow torch

Serves 12

Preheat the oven to 180°C/350°F/Gas 4.

Fold the lemon zest into the cake batter. Spoon one-third of the mixture into one of the prepared cake pans. Add a few drops of yellow food colouring to the remaining batter and whisk in. Spoon half of the yellow batter into the second cake pan. Add a further few drops of food colouring to the remaining batter to make a darker yellow colour, and spoon it into the final cake pan. Bake in the preheated oven for 25–30 minutes, until the cakes spring back to the touch and a knife inserted into the centre of each cake comes out clean.

For the drizzle, heat the lemon juice and icing/confectioners' sugar in a saucepan and bring to the boil. Spoon one-third of the drizzle over the top of each cake while still warm, then leave to cool in the pans.

For the buttercream filling, whisk together the icing/confectioners' sugar and butter until you have a smooth, stiff icing, adding a little milk if the mixture is too stiff.

Trim away the edges of each cake using a sharp knife if you wish to expose the colour of each sponge. Place the darkest yellow cake on a cake stand and spread over half of the buttercream. Add a tablespoon of lemon curd and spread out over the buttercream. Top with the middle yellow cake and repeat the buttercream and lemon curd filling. Top with the final cake.

To make the Italian meringue, heat the sugar, syrup and 3 tablespoons of water in a saucepan until the sugar has dissolved, then bring to the boil. In a large bowl, whisk the egg whites with a balloon whisk or mixer to stiff peaks. Gradually pour the hot sugar syrup into the egg whites in a thin stream and whisk until the meringue cools slightly. This is best done with a stand mixer. Spoon the meringue into the piping/pastry bag and pipe peaks of meringue over the top of the cake. Lightly brown the meringue with a chef's blow torch.

Serve the cake straight away. This cake is best eaten on the day it is made due to the meringue topping.

Caramel layer cake

This cake is a toffee lover's delight as it contains sponges flavoured with the molasses taste of dark brown sugar and a caramel glaze on each layer, all sandwiched with naughty clotted cream. This cake is decorated with pretty violas, but if you do not have any you can replace them with caramel or chocolate curls instead.

340 g/1¾ cups soft dark brown sugar

340 g/3 sticks butter, softened

6 eggs

340 g/2½ cups self-raising/self-rising flour, sifted

2 tablespoons sour cream

edible flowers, such as violas or gerbera petals, to decorate

FOR THE CARAMEL GLAZE

50 g/3½ tablespoons butter

100 g/½ cup caster/superfine sugar

125 ml/½ cup double/heavy cream

80 g/generous ½ cup fondant icing/confectioners' sugar, sifted

FOR THE FILLING

225 g/8 oz. clotted cream (or 300 ml/1¼ cups double/heavy cream, whipped to stiff peaks)

3 x 20-cm/8-inch round cake pans, greased and lined with baking parchment

Serves 12

Preheat the oven to 180°C (350°F) Gas 4.

For the cake, whisk together the sugar and butter until light and creamy. Whisk in the eggs one at a time. Fold in the flour and sour cream and divide the mixture equally between the prepared cake pans. Bake for 25–30 minutes until they are golden brown and spring back to the touch and a knife inserted into the centre of each cake comes out clean. Slide a knife around the edge of each cake and let cool in the pans for a few minutes, then turn out onto a wire rack to cool completely.

For the caramel glaze, heat the butter and caster/superfine sugar in a saucepan until the butter and sugar have melted and the mixture starts to caramelize. Add the cream and simmer until you have a golden caramel. The mixture may spit as you add the cream so take care when pouring it in. Do not worry if lumps of sugar form on adding the cream, as these will melt, or the mixture can be passed through a sieve/fine mesh strainer. Sift the icing/confectioners' sugar into the caramel and beat until smooth, then leave to cool slightly.

Spoon the cooled caramel glaze over the top of each cake on the wire rack, with a sheet of foil underneath to catch any drips. Spread half of the clotted cream on top of two of the cakes, then stack the cakes on a serving plate, placing the caramel-only layer on top. Decorate with edible flowers. If you use whole flowers to decorate, these will not be edible (the stems and inner part of the flower are very bitter), so they are for decorative purposes only and should be removed as you cut the cake. Never eat floral decorations unless you are certain it is safe to do so.

Serve immediately or store in the refrigerator until you are ready to serve. As the cake contains fresh cream, it is best eaten on the day it is made, although it will keep for up to 2 days in the refrigerator.

Naked fancies

While traditional fondant fancies are covered in a layer of glossy icing, these fancies are positively 'nude' with a translucent icing that is almost invisible and lets you see the cake and buttercream layers below. Decorated with crystallized flowers, these are a perfect treat for afternoon tea. If you do not have violet liqueur, you can use other liqueurs of your choosing – Cointreau or Grand Marnier both work well.

1 recipe 2-egg Cake Batter
(see page 9)

40 ml/3 tablespoons violet
liqueur, to drizzle

crystallized flowers or petals,
such as violets, to decorate

edible glitter (optional)

FOR THE BUTTERCREAM

300 g/generous 2 cups icing/
confectioners' sugar

30 g/2 tablespoons butter,
softened

1–2 tablespoons milk
(if needed)

FOR THE FONDANT GLAZE

280 g/2 cups fondant
icing/confectioners' sugar,
sifted

50 ml/3½ tablespoons violet
liqueur

*a 20-cm/8-inch square cake pan,
greased and lined with baking
parchment*

Makes 16

Preheat the oven to 180°C (350°F) Gas 4.

Spoon the cake batter into the prepared cake pan and bake in the preheated oven for 20–25 minutes, until the cake is golden brown and springs back to the touch and a knife inserted into the centre of the cake comes out clean. Let cool in the pan for a few minutes, then turn out onto a wire rack to cool completely.

For the buttercream, whisk together the icing/confectioners' sugar and butter until light and creamy, adding a little milk if the mixture is too stiff.

Cut the cake in half horizontally using a large serrated knife. Place the bottom half of the cake on a chopping board or tray that is small enough to fit in the refrigerator. Drizzle the violet liqueur over the cake and spread over a thin layer of the buttercream. Top with the second cake half and cover the top in a thin layer of buttercream. Chill in the refrigerator for 2 hours, until the buttercream is set firm. Trim the edges of the cake, then cut the cake into 16 even squares.

To make the fondant glaze, heat the fondant icing/confectioners' sugar in a saucepan with the violet liqueur and about 100 ml/generous ⅓ cup water. You need a thin icing, so add the water gradually until it is runny and almost translucent.

Spoon the warm icing over the cakes, making sure that each cake is covered completely, or dip the cakes into the icing to coat them, taking care that it is not too hot. Place the covered cakes on a wire rack with foil underneath to catch the icing drips.

Decorate the tops of the cakes with crystallized flowers or petals and dust with edible glitter for a shimmer effect, if you like.

This cake will keep for up to 2 days stored in an airtight container.

Chocolate peppermint roulade with frosted mint leaves

This elegant roulade is decorated only with a dusting of cocoa powder and some simple frosted mint leaves. It makes a chic and impressive dessert.

150 ml/⅔ cup milk

40 g/generous ¼ cup self-raising/self-rising flour, sifted

5 eggs, separated

100 g/½ cup caster/granulated sugar

100 g/3½ oz. peppermint-flavoured plain/bittersweet chocolate, melted

350 ml/1½ cups double/heavy cream

icing/confectioners' sugar and unsweetened cocoa powder, for dusting

FOR THE FROSTED MINT LEAVES

fresh mint leaves

1 egg white

caster/superfine sugar, for sprinkling

a paint brush

a baking sheet, lined with a silicone mat or baking parchment

a 38 x 28-cm/15 x 11-inch Swiss roll/jelly roll pan, greased and lined with baking parchment

Serves 6–8

Begin by preparing the frosted mint leaves. Whisk the egg white until very foamy. Using a paint brush, paint the egg white on both the front and the back of each leaf and sprinkle with sugar so that each leaf is coated in a thin layer. Place on the prepared baking sheet and set aside until needed. You can also leave them in a warm place to dry overnight, then store them in an airtight container until needed.

Preheat the oven to 200°C (400°F) Gas 6.

For the roulade, heat the milk and flour together in a saucepan over low heat, and whisk to a smooth paste. In a large mixing bowl, whisk the egg yolks and sugar together until thick, creamy and voluminous. Beat the flour mixture into the sugar and eggs, then beat in the melted chocolate.

In a separate bowl, whisk the egg whites to stiff peaks. Adding one-third at a time, fold the egg whites into the roulade batter. Pour the mixture into the prepared Swiss roll/jelly roll pan and spread out evenly. Bake for 8–12 minutes until the sponge springs back to the touch.

Lay a sheet of non-stick baking parchment, larger than the size of the pan, on a flat surface. Dust with icing/confectioners' sugar and cocoa powder. Remove the roulade from the oven and turn out onto the dusted parchment. Remove the lining paper, then roll the sponge up using the dusted parchment, with the parchment rolled inside the roulade. Let cool completely.

When you are ready to serve, whip the cream to stiff peaks. Unroll the roulade. Using a spatula, spread a layer of cream over the sponge, then roll up the roulade. Place on a serving plate and dust with a little extra cocoa powder. Decorate with the frosted mint leaves and serve straight away.

Serve straight away or store in the refrigerator until you are ready to serve. As the cake contains fresh cream, it is best eaten on the day it is made, although it will keep for up to 2 days in the refrigerator.

Coconut angel cake with raspberries

Angel cake is a fatless sponge made without any egg yolks, and is therefore perfectly white inside when you cut into it. Traditionally it is cooked in an angel cake pan – which has straight sides and a funnel in the middle – but you can cook the cake in a Bundt pan if you do not have one. This version has a coconut icing and fresh raspberries on top, and sweetened coconut in the sponge.

140 g/generous 1 cup plain/
all-purpose flour

100 g/¾ cup icing/
confectioners' sugar

8 egg whites

100 g/½ cup caster/
granulated sugar

a pinch of salt

1 teaspoon cream of tartar

80 g/generous 1 cup long
shredded sweetened coconut
or desiccated/dried
unsweetened coconut

FOR THE ICING

30 ml/⅛ cup coconut cream

150 g/1 cup icing/confectioners'
sugar

TO DECORATE

30 g/½ cup long shredded
coconut or shavings of
fresh coconut

300 g/10½ oz. (about 3¼ cups)
raspberries

icing/confectioners' sugar,
for dusting

*a 25-cm/10-inch angel cake pan,
greased*

Serves 8

Preheat the oven to 180°C (350°F) Gas 4.

Sift the flour and icing/confectioners' sugar together and set aside. In a clean mixing bowl, whisk the egg whites to stiff peaks. Whisk in the caster/granulated sugar, a spoonful at a time, then add the salt and cream of tartar. Carefully fold in the flour and icing/confectioners' sugar mixture and the coconut, folding gently with a spatula to retain as much air in the mixture as possible. Spoon the mixture into the prepared cake pan and bake for 30–35 minutes until the cake is golden brown and firm to the touch and a knife inserted into the centre of the cake comes out clean. Carefully slide a knife around the edges of the cake before releasing it from the pan to ensure it does not stick, then turn out onto a wire rack to cool completely.

In a dry frying pan/skillet set over low heat, toast the coconut for decoration until lightly golden brown. The coconut can burn easily, so watch it very carefully and as it starts to turn colour tip it onto a clean plate immediately to prevent it cooking further in the hot pan.

For the icing, mix together the coconut cream and icing/confectioners' sugar to a smooth, thick icing. Spread over the top of the cake. Top the cake with the raspberries and toasted coconut and dust with icing/confectioners' sugar.

This cake is best eaten on the day it is made.

Naked Battenberg

I have always loved Battenberg cake with its pretty squares of yellow and pink sponge. Traditionally wrapped in marzipan, it is not a cake that everyone enjoys as some people do not like marzipan. This 'naked' version is coated in an almond buttercream and toasted almonds in place of the marzipan and proved very popular when I served it. A Battenberg cake pan is divided into 4 equal rectangles so that you get perfectly equal squares when you slice the cake, and is worth investing in if you make Battenberg cakes regularly. If you do not have one, simply use two loaf pans to cook the two different coloured cake batters, then cut each into two rectangles. It is important that the pans are the same size so that you end up with 4 equal rectangles.

1 teaspoon vanilla bean paste or pure vanilla extract

1 recipe 2-egg Cake Batter (see page 9)

pink food colouring

100 g/1¼ cups toasted flaked/slivered almonds, finely chopped

FOR THE BUTTERCREAM

115 g/generous ¾ cup icing/confectioners' sugar, sifted

1 tablespoon butter, softened

1 tablespoon almond butter

a little milk (if needed)

a 20 x 15-cm/8 x 6-inch Battenberg cake pan (or 2 loaf pans, 20 x 8 cm/8 x 3 inches), greased and lined with baking parchment

Serves 8

Preheat the oven to 180°C (350°F) Gas 4.

Fold the vanilla into the cake batter and divide the mixture equally between two bowls. Add a few drops of pink food colouring to one of the bowls and fold in. Divide the cake batters between the sections of the prepared cake pan so that you have two plain and two pink rectangles of cake. (If using the loaf pans, cook the pink cake batter in one pan and the plain cake batter in the other.) Bake for 20–25 minutes until the cakes spring back to the touch and a knife inserted into the centre of each rectangle of cake comes out clean. Leave the cakes to cool completely in the pan, then remove them carefully. Trim the cakes if necessary (for example, if one of the cakes has risen more than the others), so that you have 4 equal-sized rectangles of cake.

For the buttercream, whisk together the icing/confectioners' sugar, butter and almond butter until you have a smooth, stiff icing, adding a little milk if the mixture is too stiff.

Using a knife, spread a little of the buttercream onto the top of one of the pink rectangles and place a plain rectangle on top. Repeat with the remaining two rectangles, but this time place the plain cake on the bottom. Spread the side of one of the pairs with a little buttercream and sandwich the two pairs of cake together so that when you look at the end of the cake the pink and plain squares are diagonally opposite one another. Carefully spread the buttercream in a thin layer over the outside of the cake, taking care as the cake is fragile. Put the flaked/slivered almonds on a plate and gently roll the cake in the almonds, pressing them onto the buttercream with your hands. Wrap the cake in a layer of clingfilm/plastic wrap and leave to set in the fridge for about 2 hours. Remove the cake from the clingfilm/plastic wrap and place on a serving plate.

This cake will keep for up to 2 days stored in an airtight container.

Naked brownie stack

These decadent brownies are rich and chocolatey and look so pretty piled high on a cake stand decorated with dried berry pieces or petals.

250 g/2¼ sticks butter

350 g/12½ oz. plain/bittersweet chocolate, chopped

5 eggs

200 g/1 cup caster/granulated sugar

200 g/1 cup soft dark brown sugar

200 g/1½ cups plain/all-purpose flour, sifted

200 g/7 oz. white chocolate, chopped

1 tablespoon rose syrup

To decorate

unsweetened cocoa powder, for dusting

freeze-dried raspberry and strawberry pieces or edible dried petals

a 38 x 28-cm/15 x 11-inch baking pan, greased and lined with baking parchment

Makes 24

Put the butter and plain/bittersweet chocolate in a heatproof bowl set over a pan of simmering water, making sure the bottom of the bowl does not touch the water. Stir occasionally until the chocolate and butter are melted and you have a smooth glossy sauce. If you are short of time, you can do this in a microwave by heating the butter and chocolate on full power for 40 seconds, stirring, then heating for a further 20–30 seconds or so until both the butter and chocolate have melted. Leave the mixture to cool.

Preheat the oven to 180°C (350°F) Gas 4.

In a large mixing bowl, whisk together the eggs and both sugars until the mixture is thick and creamy and has doubled in size. Pour in the melted chocolate mixture and whisk again. Add the flour, chopped white chocolate and rose syrup and fold in gently using a spatula. Spoon the mixture into the prepared baking pan and bake in the preheated oven for 30–35 minutes, until a crust has formed on top but the brownie still feels a little soft underneath. Let cool completely in the pan, then turn out and cut into 24 squares.

Decorate the brownies with a dusting of cocoa powder and some freeze-dried raspberry and strawberry pieces or edible dried petals. Stack the brownies on a cake stand or plate to serve.

The brownies will keep for up to 5 days stored in an airtight container.

Salty honey cake

This cake is inspired by one of my favourite pies from Four and Twenty Blackbirds Bakery in Brooklyn, New York, where my brother lives. I adore the sweet and salty combination of salt and honey. Vanilla salt is infused with vanilla seeds and is wonderful for cakes. If you want to make your own, fill a jar with sea salt flakes and the seeds of several vanilla pods/beans (and the pods/beans themselves), shake well to disperse the seeds and then leave to infuse for several weeks before using.

2 tablespoons runny honey

**a pinch of vanilla salt
(or sea salt plus 1 teaspoon
vanilla extract)**

**1 recipe 5-egg Cake Batter
(see page 9)**

FOR THE SALTY HONEY GLAZE

2 tablespoons runny honey

50 g/3½ tablespoons butter

**a pinch of vanilla salt
(or sea salt plus 1 teaspoon
vanilla extract)**

*a 26-cm/10½-inch ring Bundt
pan, greased*

Serves 10

Preheat the oven to 180°C (350°F) Gas 4.

Whisk the honey and vanilla salt into the cake batter and spoon into the prepared Bundt pan. Bake in the preheated oven for 45–60 minutes, until the cake is golden brown and springs back to the touch and a knife inserted into the centre of the cake comes out clean. Allow to cool completely in the pan, then gently prise the cake from the pan, sliding a knife around the centre well to ease it out.

For the glaze, heat the honey and butter in a saucepan over low heat until the butter has melted, then stir in the vanilla. Spoon the glaze over the top of the cake and leave to set before serving.

This cake will keep for up to 2 days stored in an airtight container.

Rustic cheesecake tower

This cheesecake is plain and simple, yet looks spectacular piled with summer berries and wild strawberries and their flowers. It would make a great alternative wedding cake. You can add flavourings to the cheesecake cream if you wish, such as citrus zest or chocolate chips, or even rum-soaked raisins.

FOR THE BASE

400 g/14 oz. digestive biscuits/graham crackers

200 g/1¾ sticks butter, melted

FOR THE FILLING

750 ml/3 cups crème fraîche/sour cream

5 eggs

200 g/1 cup caster/granulated sugar

800 g/1¾ lb. cream cheese

3 tablespoons plain/all-purpose flour, sifted

1 vanilla pod/bean

TO DECORATE

fresh berries and food-safe, pesticide-free strawberry leaves and flowers

icing/confectioners' sugar

18-cm/7-inch and 26-cm/10½-inch round springform cake pans, greased and lined with baking parchment

Serves 15

Preheat the oven to 170°C (325°F) Gas 3.

Crush the biscuits/crackers to fine crumbs in a food processor, or put in a clean plastic bag and bash with a rolling pin. Transfer to a mixing bowl and stir in the melted butter, then press into the base of the prepared pans firmly using the back of a spoon. Wrap the base and sides of the pans in several layers of clingfilm/plastic wrap and place in a large roasting pan full of water to come halfway up the sides of the pan.

For the filling, whisk together the crème fraîche/sour cream, eggs, sugar, cream cheese and flour. Using a sharp knife, split the vanilla pod/bean in half, scrape out the seeds from both halves of the pod/bean and add to the cheesecake mixture. Whisk until the seeds are evenly distributed.

Pour the mixture into the pans, adding approximately two-thirds of the mixture to the large pan and one-third to the smaller pan. Bake for 1–1¼ hours, until golden brown on top but still with a slight wobble in the centre. Leave to cool in the pans, then transfer to the refrigerator to chill for at least 3 hours, or preferably overnight.

To serve, remove the cheesecakes from their pans and place the large cheesecake on a serving plate. Place the small cheesecake in the centre on top. Decorate with fresh berries and food-safe flowers, and dust with a little icing/confectioners' sugar to serve.

This cheesecake will keep for up to 3 days stored in the refrigerator.

Vintage Elegance

Bunting cake

I am not ashamed to admit that I love bunting. I have it hanging in most rooms of my cottage and in my garden and this is therefore one of my favourite cakes! You can make the bunting in advance using small pieces of coloured decorative paper or even fabric if you want your cake to be extra special. This cake could be made in a larger size with tiers for a wedding, if you wish.

½ teaspoon vanilla bean powder or 1 teaspoon pure vanilla extract

1 recipe 6-egg Cake Batter (see page 9)

225 g/8 oz. clotted cream (or 300 ml/1¼ cups double/heavy cream, whipped to stiff peaks)

4 tablespoons strawberry jam/jelly

icing/confectioners' sugar, for dusting

food-safe, pesticide-free flowers, such as carnations, to decorate

3 x 20-cm/8-inch round cake pans, greased and lined with baking parchment

2 wooden skewers

a needle and thread

decorative fabric or paper

sellotape

Serves 12

Preheat the oven to 180°C (350°F) Gas 4.

Fold the vanilla into the cake batter and divide the mixture equally between the prepared cake pans. Bake in the preheated oven for 25–30 minutes, until the cakes are golden brown and spring back to the touch and a knife inserted into the centre of each cake comes out clean. Leave to cool in the pans for a few minutes, then turn out onto a wire rack to cool completely.

To prepare the bunting, cut small triangles of the coloured fabric or paper and, using the needle, sew them onto the thread so that they hang like bunting. Fix the thread to the top of the skewers by tying in a knot.

When you are ready to serve, place one of the cakes on a serving plate or cake stand. Spread half of the clotted cream over the cake and top with 2 tablespoons of the jam. Top with a second cake and spread over the remaining clotted cream and jam. Finish the stack with the third cake and dust with icing/confectioners' sugar. Insert the skewers into the top of the cake, pressing them down until they feel secure and the bunting hangs prettily over the cake. Arrange the fresh flowers in the centre of the cake. The flowers are for decorative purposes only and should be removed as you cut the cake. Never eat floral decorations unless you are certain it is safe to do so.

Serve straight away or store in the refrigerator until you are ready to serve. As the cake contains fresh cream, it is best eaten on the day it is made, although it will keep for up to 2 days in the refrigerator.

Earl Grey tea cake

There are few more refreshing drinks than a steaming hot cup of Earl Grey tea, with its delicious bergamot citrus flavours. The fruit in this cake is infused with Earl Grey and is great to serve in the afternoon with a cup of your favourite tea. If you want, you can add pretty dried blue cornflower petals to the cake batter.

1 Earl Grey tea bag

1 tablespoon honey

300 g/2 generous cups sultanas/golden raisins

80 g/generous ⅓ cup caster/granulated sugar

2 eggs

grated zest of 1 lemon

280 g/2 generous cups self-raising/self-rising flour, sifted

1 tablespoon dried cornflower petals (optional)

icing/confectioners' sugar, for dusting

a 23-cm/9-inch square cake pan, greased and lined with baking parchment

Serves 8

Begin by soaking the fruit. Pour 250 ml/1 cup boiling water over the tea bag in a bowl and leave to steep for 2–3 minutes. Remove the tea bag and add the honey and sultanas. Leave to soak for 2–3 hours until the fruit is plump. Strain the fruit, reserving the tea as this will be added to the cake batter later.

Preheat the oven to 180°C (350°F) Gas 4.

Whisk together the sugar and eggs until thick and creamy. Stir in the drained fruit, lemon zest, flour and petals, if using. Pour in the reserved tea, whisking all the time. Spoon the mixture into the prepared cake pan and bake for 45–60 minutes, until the cake is golden brown and a knife inserted into the centre of the cake comes out clean. Leave to cool in the pan for a few minutes, then turn out onto a wire rack to cool completely. Alternatively, you can serve the cake still warm, if you wish.

To serve, simply dust with icing/confectioners' sugar. Place a doily on top of the cake before dusting, if you want to create a pretty pattern with the sugar.

This cake will keep for up to 3 days stored in an airtight container.

Flower garden timbale cakes

These little cakes are very simple, just flavoured with vanilla and dusted with sugar. They do, however, look so elegant stacked on cake stands and topped with fresh edible flowers, and would make a perfect wedding cake. You can scale the quantities up or down depending on how many cakes you need to make and can also flavour the batter with a little citrus zest or rose water in place of the vanilla, if you wish. If you do not have 24 dariole moulds, you can bake the batter in batches, washing and regreasing the moulds between each batch.

1 teaspoon vanilla bean powder or 2 teaspoons pure vanilla extract

1 recipe 6-egg Cake Batter (see page 9)

icing/confectioners' sugar, for dusting

edible flowers or crystallized petals, to decorate

24 dariole moulds, greased and set on a baking sheet

a piping/pastry bag fitted with large round nozzle/tip (optional)

Makes 24

Preheat the oven to 180°C (350°F) Gas 4.

Fold the vanilla into the cake batter. Spoon the mixture into the piping/pastry bag and pipe the batter into the cake moulds. If you prefer, you can do this using small spoons instead, although I find that it is easier and neater if you use a piping/pastry bag. Bake the cakes in the preheated oven for 20–30 minutes, until they are golden brown and spring back to the touch. Leave to cool for a few minutes in the moulds, then slide a knife around the edge of each mould and turn the cakes out onto a wire rack and leave to cool completely.

Dust the top and sides of each cake liberally with icing/confectioners' sugar and top with a fresh, edible flower. Whole flowers are best removed before eating, as the stalks can have a bitter taste, so they are really for decorative purposes only. Alternatively, use crystallized edible petals instead. Never eat floral decorations unless you are certain it is safe to do so.

These cakes will keep for up to 2 days stored in an airtight container.

Macaron cake

This pretty cake would not be out of place in the window of a fine French pâtisserie store, filled with fresh berries and topped with sugar macarons.

1 recipe 6-egg Cake Batter (see page 9)

pink food colouring paste

FOR THE MACARONS

130 g/1⅓ cups ground almonds

180 g/scant 1 cup icing/confectioners' sugar

3 egg whites

80 g/⅓ cup plus 1 tablespoon caster/superfine sugar

pink food colouring paste

FOR THE FILLING

450 g/1 lb. clotted cream (or 600 ml/2½ cups double/heavy cream, whipped to stiff peaks)

300 g/3 cups strawberries, hulled and sliced

2 tablespoons strawberry jam/jelly

300 g/2 generous cups raspberries

2 tablespoons raspberry jam/jelly

icing/confectioners' sugar, for dusting

food-safe fresh leaves, such as mint or bay leaves

a piping/pastry bag fitted with large round nozzle/tip

2 baking sheets, lined with silicone mats

3 x 20-cm/8-inch round cake pans, greased and lined with baking parchment

Serves 12

Begin by preparing the macarons. Put the ground almonds and icing/confectioners' sugar in a food processor and blitz to a fine powder. Sift the nut powder into a bowl, returning any pieces that do not pass through the sieve/strainer to the blender. Blitz, then sift again.

In a clean mixing bowl, whisk the egg whites to stiff peaks, then, continuing to whisk, add the caster/superfine sugar, a spoonful at a time, until the meringue is smooth and glossy. Add the food colouring paste, then add the nut powder, one-third at a time, folding in with a spatula. As you fold, the colour will become even. It is very important to get the meringue to the right texture; it needs to be folded until it is just soft enough that it will not quite hold a peak. Drop a little of the mixture onto a plate; if it settles into a smooth surface, it is ready. If it holds a peak then you need to fold it a few more times. If you fold it too much it will be too runny and the macarons will not hold their shape.

Spoon the mixture into a piping/pastry bag. Pipe 3-cm/1¼-inch circles onto the prepared baking sheets, spacing them out well as they will spread during cooking. Leave the macarons on the sheets for 1 hour, so that a skin forms. Meanwhile, preheat the oven to 160°C (325°F) Gas 3.

Bake the macarons for 20–30 minutes, until firm, then let cool completely on the baking sheets. Turn the oven up to 180°C (350°F) Gas 4.

Spoon one-third of the cake batter into one of the cake pans. Divide the remaining cake batter into two bowls and colour one portion pale pink and the other portion a deeper pink. Transfer to the remaining pans. Bake for 25–30 minutes, until the cakes spring back to the touch and a knife inserted into the centre of each cake comes out clean. Let cool in the pans for a few minutes, then turn out onto a wire rack to cool completely.

Trim away the edges of the cakes to reveal the coloured sponge. Place the deep pink cake on a serving plate and spread with a generous layer of clotted cream. Top with the strawberries, then spoon over the strawberry jam. Top with the pale pink cake and cover with more cream, most of the raspberries and then the raspberry jam. Top with the plain cake and dust with icing/confectioners' sugar.

Sandwich 8–10 pairs of macarons together with a little of the cream. (Store the remaining macarons in an airtight container to eat another day.) Decorate the cake with macarons, raspberries and leaves. Serve straight away or store in the refrigerator until you are ready to serve. As the cake contains fresh cream, it is best eaten on the day it is made, although it will keep for up to 2 days in the refrigerator.

Crystallized flower garden cake

This is one of my favourite cakes as it is so simple and yet very elegant. To me it has a very vintage feel and would not have been out of place in an afternoon tea served in Victorian times. You can use any edible flowers and leaves you wish to decorate – violas, primroses, verbena flowers and leaves, pansies and mint leaves all work well.

grated zest and freshly squeezed juice of 1 orange

1 recipe 5-egg Cake Batter (see page 9)

225 g/8 oz. clotted cream (or 300 ml/1¼ cups double/heavy cream, whipped to stiff peaks)

2 tablespoons blackcurrant jam/jelly

icing/confectioners' sugar, for dusting

40 g/1½ oz. white chocolate, melted

FOR THE SUGAR FLOWERS

1 egg white

pesticide-free, edible flowers, such as pansies, violas, lemon verbena flowers (or edible leaves, such as mint leaves and lemon verbena leaves)

caster/superfine sugar, for sprinkling

a paint brush

a baking sheet, lined with a silicone mat or baking parchment

2 x 20-cm/8-inch round cake pans, greased and lined with baking parchment

Serves 8

Begin by preparing the crystallized sugar flowers , as they need to dry overnight. Whisk the egg white until very foamy. Using a paint brush, carefully paint the egg white on both the front and the back of the flowers and leaves and sprinkle with sugar so that the whole leaf or flower is coated in a thin layer of sugar. This is best done by holding the sugar just above the flower and sprinkling. Have a plate below to catch the excess sugar. Repeat with all the flowers and leaves, covering them one at a time, and place them on the prepared baking sheet. Leave in a warm place to dry overnight. Once dried, store the petals in an airtight container until you are ready to serve.

Preheat the oven to 180°C (350°F) Gas 4.

Fold the orange zest and juice into the cake batter and divide the mixture equally between the prepared cake pans. Bake in the preheated oven for 25–30 minutes, until the cakes are golden brown and they spring back to the touch and a knife comes out clean when inserted into the centre of each cake. Leave to cool in the pans for a few minutes, then turn out onto a wire rack to cool completely.

When you are ready to serve, place one of the cakes on a cake stand. Spread with the clotted cream and spoon the jam on the top. Spread out the jam carefully using a knife. Place the second cake on top and dust with a good layer of icing/confectioners' sugar. Fix the crystallized flowers and leaves on top of the cake in a pretty pattern using a little of the melted white chocolate.

Serve straight away or store in the refrigerator until you are ready to serve. As the cake contains fresh cream, it is best eaten on the day it is made, although it will keep for up to 2 days in the refrigerator.

Rose and violet cake

I always remember eating rose and violet cream chocolates with my grandma. They were her favourite and, as I have grown older, they have become favourites of mine too. This cake has a rose sponge and a violet ganache topping and is decorated with the prettiest pink and purple candied flowers. It is rich so you only need to serve small slices.

1 tablespoon rosewater

1 recipe 4-egg Cake Batter (see page 9)

candied rose and violet petals, to decorate

FOR THE VIOLET GANACHE

2 eggs

375 ml/1½ cups double/heavy cream

125 ml/½ cup milk

300 g/10½ oz. plain/bittersweet chocolate (minimum 70% cocoa solids)

60 ml/¼ cup violet liqueur

a 23-cm/9-inch loose-bottomed deep cake pan, greased and lined with baking parchment

Serves 12

Preheat the oven to 180°C (350°F) Gas 4.

Fold the rosewater into the cake batter and spoon the mixture into the prepared cake pan. Bake in the preheated oven for 25–30 minutes, until the cake is golden brown and springs back to the touch and a knife inserted into the centre of the cake comes out clean. Leave the cake to cool in the pan.

For the violet ganache, whisk the eggs, cream and milk together. Break the chocolate into small pieces and put in a saucepan with the cream mixture and the violet liqueur. Heat over gentle heat, stirring all the time, for about 4–5 minutes until the chocolate is melted and the ganache is thick and glossy. Pour over the cake and chill in the refrigerator overnight until the ganache has set. If the seal of your pan is not tight, wrap the base and side of the pan in kitchen foil to ensure that the ganache does not leak out of the pan.

When you are ready to serve, remove the cake from the pan by sliding a sharp knife around the edge, then remove the sides. Place the cake on a serving plate and sprinkle with the candied rose and violet petals to decorate. You can make pretty flower patterns using the violet petals with a small crystallized rose piece in the centre.

This cake will keep for up to 3 days stored in the refrigerator, although you should only put the petals on just before serving.

Summer flower ring cake

Sometimes all you need to create a spectacular naked cake is a decorative cake pan. A dusting of powdered sugar will show off the pattern from the pan beautifully.

1 heaped tablespoon lemon curd

grated zest of 2 lemons

1 recipe 5-egg Cake Batter (see page 9)

freshly squeezed juice of 2 lemons

2 tablespoons icing/confectioners' sugar

TO DECORATE

icing/confectioners' sugar, for dusting

food-safe, pesticide-free flowers, such as chrysanthemums

a 25-cm/10-inch Bundt pan, greased

Serves 10

Preheat the oven to 180°C (350°F) Gas 4.

Fold the lemon curd and zest into the cake batter using a spatula and spoon into the prepared Bundt pan. Bake in the preheated oven for 40–50 minutes until it springs back to the touch and a knife inserted into the centre of the cake comes out clean. Let cool completely in the pan, then carefully prize the cake away from the sides of the pan by sliding a knife around the centre ring. Turn the cake out onto a serving plate by holding the plate over the pan tightly and inverting it.

Heat the lemon juice and icing/confectioners' sugar in a saucepan over a gentle heat, until the sugar has dissolved and you have a lemon syrup. Spoon over the top of the cake.

Dust the cake with icing/confectioners' sugar and decorate with the flowers. The flowers are for decorative purposes only and should be removed as you cut the cake. Never eat floral decorations unless you are certain it is safe to do so.

This cake will keep for up to 3 days stored in an airtight container.

Lime charlotte cake

A traditional charlotte makes such a pretty centrepiece dessert, tied with ribbons and topped with glistening berries. This lime sponge is topped with a tangy lime mousse, piled high with ripe and juicy berries.

grated zest of 2 limes

1 recipe 2-egg Cake Batter (see page 9)

200 g/7 oz. sponge finger biscuits/ladyfinger cookies

300 g/10½ oz. strawberries

icing/confectioners' sugar, for dusting

FOR THE FILLING

freshly squeezed juice of 3 limes

grated zest of 1 lime

300 g/1⅓ cups cream cheese

200 g/scant 1 cup sweetened condensed milk

a 16-cm/6½-inch loose-bottomed deep cake pan, greased and lined with baking parchment

a pretty ribbon

Serves 8

Preheat the oven to 180°C (350°F) Gas 4.

Fold the lime zest into the cake batter and spoon into the prepared cake pan. Bake in the preheated oven for 20–30 minutes, until the cake is golden brown and springs back to the touch and a knife inserted into the centre of the cake comes out clean. Let cool in the pan.

For the filling, put the lime juice and zest, cream cheese and condensed milk in a mixing bowl and whisk together until thick and creamy. Spoon the mousse on top of the cooled cake and chill in the refrigerator for at least 3 hours, or preferably overnight, until the mousse has set.

When you are ready to serve, slide a knife around the edge of the pan and remove the sides. Remove the pan base and lining paper and place the cake on a serving plate. Carefully press the sponge fingers/ladyfingers into the sides of the cake. They should hold in place as they will stick to the mousse. Once you have placed the fingers in a ring around the cake, tie the ribbon around the cake to hold them firmly in place.

Remove most of the stalks of the strawberries, but leave a few in place for a pretty red and green contrast. Place the strawberries on top of the charlotte, arranging the ones with stalks at the top. Dust with icing/confectioners' sugar and serve.

This cake will keep for up to 3 days stored in the refrigerator, but should only be assembled just before serving as the sponge fingers will become soft over time.

Mini Victoria layer cakes

One of my favourite cakes is a classic sandwich cake. In fact, I don't know anyone who will refuse a slice of Victoria sponge! These cakes are my mini version, and are elegantly topped with rose buds and sandwiched together with cream and jam. You can replace the cream with classic buttercream if you prefer, although I find fresh cream gives a lighter, less-sweet finish to these little cakes. The rose buds are for decoration only and should not be eaten. If you want to serve an edible decoration, top with crystallized rose petals instead (see page 26).

1 teaspoon vanilla extract

1 recipe 2-egg Cake Batter (see page 9)

300 ml/1¼ cups double/ heavy cream

4 tablespoons raspberry jam/jelly

icing/confectioners' sugar, for dusting

8 food-safe, pesticide-free mini rose buds

8 x 6.5-cm/2½-inch cake rings, greased and placed on a greased baking sheet

2 piping/pastry bags fitted with large round nozzles/tips

Makes 8

Preheat the oven to 180°C (350°F) Gas 4.

Fold the vanilla into the cake batter and divide the mixture equally between the prepared cake rings. You can do this either by spooning the batter in, or by putting the batter in a piping/pastry bag and piping it in neatly. Bake in the preheated oven for 15–20 minutes, until the cakes are golden brown and spring back to the touch. Leave the cakes to cool in the rings for a few minutes, then remove by sliding a sharp knife around the inside of each ring. Transfer the cakes to a wire rack and leave to cool completely.

When you are ready to serve, whip the cream to stiff peaks using a whisk. Spoon the cream into the piping/pastry bag with a round nozzle/tip. Cut each cake into thirds horizontally using a large serrated knife. Spoon a little jam/jelly onto the bottom third of each cake and then pipe a swirl of cream on top. Top each with the middle slice of cake and a little more jam/jelly and cream. Finish each cake with the cake top and dust with icing/confectioners' sugar. Pipe a little cream on the top of each cake in the middle and fix a rose in place. The flowers are for decorative purposes only and should be removed as you cut the cake. Never eat floral decorations unless you are certain it is safe to do so.

Serve straight away or store in the refrigerator until you are ready to serve. As these cakes contain fresh cream, they are best eaten on the day they are made, although they will keep for up to 2 days in the refrigerator.

Orchard harvest sponge cake

This is a very simple cake, just with fresh fruit and cream, but tastes delicious and reminds me of the orchard harvest. Each layer is topped with sugar pearls, which add a crunchy texture to the cake. You can use almost any fruits of your choosing, just make sure they are lovely and ripe – I have used apricots, nectarines and plums, but apples, pears and cherries work very well, too.

a pinch of vanilla salt
(or 1 teaspoon pure vanilla
extract and a pinch of salt)

1 recipe 6-egg Cake Batter
(see page 9)

4 apricots

5 plums

2 peaches

2 tablespoons pearl sugar
crystals, for sprinkling

FOR THE FILLING

4 tablespoons apricot conserve
or jam/jelly

300 ml/1¼ cups double/
heavy cream

2 tablespoons plum or damson
jam/jelly

3 x 20-cm/8-inch round cake
pans, greased and lined with
baking parchment

Serves 12

Preheat the oven to 180°C (350°F) Gas 4.

Fold the vanilla salt into the cake batter and divide the mixture equally between the prepared cake pans.

Cut the apricots and plums in half and remove the stones/pits. Place the apricots, cut-side down, on top of the batter in one pan, and the plums, again cut-side down, in the other pan. Remove the stones/pits from the peaches and cut them into thick slices. Arrange the slices in circular patterns on top of the batter in the final pan. Sprinkle each cake with the pearl sugar. Bake in the preheated oven for 30–40 minutes until the cakes are golden brown and spring back to the touch, and the fruit is soft. Leave the cakes to cool in the pans as they can be fragile whilst warm due to the fruit.

When you are ready to serve, heat 2 tablespoons of the apricot conserve in a saucepan until melted. Whip the cream to stiff peaks. Choose the prettiest cake to be the top layer. Place one of the other cakes on a serving plate and brush with some of the warm apricot conserve to glaze. Spoon over half of the cream and spread out, then place small spoonfuls of the plum jam/jelly over the cream. Top with the second cake and again brush with the warm apricot conserve to glaze. Top with the remaining cream and spoonfuls of the unheated apricot conserve. Place the final cake on top and brush with the remaining warm glaze.

Serve straight away or store in the refrigerator until you are ready to serve. As the cake contains fresh cream, it is best eaten on the day it is made, although it will keep for up to 2 days in the refrigerator.

Rustic Style

Spiced pear cake

This is a very simple cake but it is delicious, with fragrant spices and delicate soft poached pears stuffed with cinnamon chocolate. This is a great cut-and-come-again cake, with the pears themselves acting as the elegant decoration, glazed with a delicious toffee sauce.

1 teaspoon ground cinnamon

1 teaspoon ground ginger

1 teaspoon ground mixed spice/apple pie spice

½ teaspoon vanilla bean powder or 1 teaspoon pure vanilla extract

¼ teaspoon ground nutmeg

1 recipe 5-egg Cake Batter (see page 9)

9 squares of plain/bittersweet cinnamon chocolate or plain/bittersweet chocolate

FOR THE PEARS

9 small ripe pears

2 tablespoons honey

80 ml/⅓ cup Madeira wine or sweet sherry

freshly squeezed juice of 1 lemon

FOR THE CARAMEL GLAZE

100 g/½ cup caster/superfine sugar

50 g/3½ tablespoons butter

200 ml/¾ cup double/heavy cream

a 25-cm/10-inch square cake pan, greased and lined with baking parchment

a melon baller

Serves 10

Begin by preparing the poached pears. Peel the pears, leaving thin lines of peel in decorative patterns, if you wish. Put the pears in a saucepan with the honey, Madeira wine, lemon juice and enough water to cover the pears. Simmer over medium heat for about 15–20 minutes, until the pears are soft. Drain and place in a bowl of cold water until the pears are cool enough for you to handle. Using the melon baller, scoop out the core of each pear from the underside, leaving the stem intact.

Preheat the oven to 180°C (350°F) Gas 4.

Fold the cinnamon, ginger, mixed spice/apple pie spice, vanilla and nutmeg into the cake batter and spoon into the prepared cake pan. Place a square of chocolate into the cavity of each pear and place the pears in the cake batter in the pan, spreading them out evenly. Bake for 30 minutes, then turn the temperature down to 150°C (300°F) Gas 2 and bake for a further 30–45 minutes, until the cake springs back to the touch and a knife inserted into the centre of the cake comes out clean. Leave to cool completely in the pan.

For the caramel glaze, heat the sugar and butter in a saucepan over a low heat until the sugar starts to caramelize. Remove from the heat and whisk in the cream, taking care as the caramel may spit. Return to the heat and whisk until you have golden caramel sauce.

Place the cake on a serving plate and glaze the top with the caramel sauce using a pastry brush. Serve any extra sauce on the side, if you wish.

This cake will keep for up to 3 days stored in an airtight container.

Banana Brazil nut caramel cakes

If you like bananas, then these mini cakes are a real treat. The batter is rich with banana purée and Brazil-nut crumbs, and the cakes are topped with caramelized Brazil nuts and sticky toffee sauce. Heaven on a plate!

1 ripe banana

freshly squeezed juice
of 1 lime

115 g/generous ½ cup
soft dark brown sugar

115 g/1 stick butter, softened

2 eggs

115 g/generous ¾ cup
self-raising/self-rising
flour, sifted

80 g/⅔ cup Brazil nuts,
ground

a pinch of salt

FOR THE CARAMEL ICING

50 g/3½ tablespoons butter

75 g/⅓ cup double/heavy cream

60 g/½ cup icing/confectioners'
sugar, sifted

FOR THE DECORATION

100 g/½ cup caster/superfine
sugar

6 whole Brazil nuts

6 mini brioche moulds, greased
and set on a baking sheet

a silicone mat or greased
baking sheet

Makes 9

Preheat the oven to 180°C (350°F) Gas 4.

Mash the banana and lime juice together with a fork until you have a smooth purée. Put the banana purée, brown sugar and butter in a large mixing bowl and whisk together until light and creamy. Whisk in the eggs, one at a time, beating after each egg is added. Using a spatula, gently fold in the flour, ground Brazil nuts and salt. Divide the mixture equally between the mini brioche moulds and bake in the preheated oven for 15–20 minutes, until the cakes are golden brown and spring back to the touch. Leave to cool for a few minutes in the moulds, then carefully use a knife to loosen the cakes from the edges of the moulds.

To prepare the decoration, heat the sugar in a saucepan over low heat until melted. Do not stir the sugar as it is cooking, but swirl the pan to ensure that it does not burn. Once the sugar has melted, carefully dip the Brazil nuts into the caramel using tongs, but take extreme care as the sugar is very hot. Place the caramelized nuts on the silicone mat or prepared baking sheet to set.

Add the butter to the pan with the remaining caramelized sugar and heat until the butter has melted. Add the cream and whisk until any lumps of sugar have dissolved and you have a smooth caramel. Stir in the icing/confectioners' sugar to thicken the icing. If there are any lumps, pass the icing through a sieve/strainer. Spoon the icing over the cakes on the wire rack, sliding a sheet of foil underneath to catch any drips. Top each cake with a whole caramelized Brazil nut.

These cakes will keep for up to 3 days stored in an airtight container, although they are best eaten on the day they are made.

Charlotte royale

This cake is so naked that the sponge itself forms the decoration. The actual quantity of mousse and cake needed will depend on the size of cake pan or bowl you use.

8 eggs

230 g/1 cup plus 2 tablespoons caster/granulated sugar, plus extra for sprinkling

a pinch of vanilla salt (or a pinch of sea salt and 1 teaspoon pure vanilla extract)

230 g/1¾ cups self-raising/self-rising flour, sifted

8 tablespoons strawberry or apricot jam

FOR THE STRAWBERRY MOUSSE

600 g/1 lb 5 oz. strawberries

200 g/1 cup caster/granulated sugar

1 vanilla pod/bean, split in half and seeds removed

2 tablespoons powdered gelatine

1 litre/4 cups double/heavy cream

2 x 40 x 28-cm/16 x 11-inch Swiss roll/jelly roll pans, greased and lined

a 26-cm/10½-inch cake pan or large bowl, approximately 10 cm/4 inches deep

a piping/pastry bag fitted with large star nozzle/tip

Serves 20

Preheat the oven to 200°C (400°F) Gas 6.

Whisk together the eggs and sugar in a large mixing bowl until thick and creamy. Add the vanilla salt and flour, and fold in very gently with a spatula to ensure that you keep as much air in the batter as possible. Divide the mixture between the Swiss/jelly roll pans and bake for 10–12 minutes each, until the sponges are golden and feel firm to the touch.

Turn each cake out onto a sheet of baking parchment sprinkled with sugar. Remove the lining paper from the sponge and leave to cool for a few minutes, then spread each of the sponges with jam. Roll up each sponge into a tight spiral from one of the longer sides and leave until completely cool, wrapped in the sugar-dusted paper. Once cool, wrap the cakes and paper with clingfilm/plastic wrap until needed.

For the mousse, reserve a handful of strawberries to serve with the cake, and hull and slice the remaining strawberries. Put the sliced strawberries in a saucepan with the sugar, vanilla pod/bean and seeds and 200 ml/¾ cup of water, and simmer over low heat for 5 minutes, or until the fruit is very soft. Remove and discard the vanilla pod/bean and pass the fruit and liquid through a sieve/strainer, pressing the fruit down with the back of a spoon. Discard any fruit pulp left in the sieve/strainer. Sprinkle the gelatine over the warm strawberry liquid and whisk in until dissolved, then let cool. Pass the mixture through a sieve/strainer to ensure that any undissolved gelatine is removed. Whisk the cream to stiff peaks, then whisk in the cooled strawberry syrup.

Line the cake pan with a triple layer of clingfilm/plastic wrap making sure that there are no gaps and leaving some clingfilm/plastic wrap hanging over the sides of the pan so that it is easy to lift the cake out once the mousse has set. Cut the Swiss/jelly rolls into slices about 1½–2 cm/½–¾ inch wide. Line the base and sides of the pan with about two-thirds of the Swiss/jelly roll slices, placing them very close together so they are completely touching and there are no gaps. You can press the slices together to make them fit or add small pieces to fill gaps.

Pour the mousse into the bowl and leave to set in the refrigerator for a few hours, or until the mousse starts to thicken. Cover the top of the mousse with the remaining slices of Swiss/jelly roll, ensuring that there are no gaps. Wrap the top of the bowl in a layer of clingfilm/plastic wrap and chill in the refrigerator overnight to let the mousse set completely.

To serve, remove the top layer of clingfilm/plastic wrap. Place a large serving plate on top of the bowl and then, holding the bowl and plate together tightly, invert the cake so that it is released from the bowl and sits on the plate. Carefully remove the layers of clingfilm/plastic wrap. Serve straight away with the reserved strawberries.

Pretty bird cake

Sometimes to make a cake spectacular, all you need is a stunning centrepiece decoration. This is a very simple chocolate cake that is transformed by the addition of a beautiful bird. You could use other rustic decorations to suit the season.

225 g/2 sticks butter, softened

225 g/generous 1 cup caster/granulated sugar

4 eggs

200 g/1½ cups self-raising/self-rising flour, sifted

60 g/generous ½ cup unsweetened cocoa powder, sifted

2 tablespoons natural/plain yogurt

a pinch of salt

FOR THE FILLING

250 g/1¾ cups icing/confectioners' sugar, sifted

2 tablespoons unsweetened cocoa powder, sifted

1 tablespoon butter, softened

1 tablespoon cream cheese

a little milk (if needed)

FOR THE GANACHE TOPPING

100 ml/generous ⅓ cup double/heavy cream

100 g/3½ oz. plain/bittersweet chocolate, broken into small pieces

1 tablespoon butter

1 tablespoon golden syrup/light corn syrup

2 x 20-cm/8-inch round cake pans, greased and lined with baking parchment

a decorative bird

Serves 8

Preheat the oven to 180°C (350°F) Gas 4.

To prepare the sponge, using a hand mixer, whisk together the butter and sugar until light and creamy. Add the eggs and whisk again. Fold in the flour, cocoa powder, yogurt and salt using a spatula until everything is incorporated. Divide the mixture equally between the prepared cake pans and bake in the preheated oven for 25–30 minutes, until the cakes spring back to the touch and a knife inserted into the centre of each cake comes out clean. Leave to cool in the pans for a few minutes, then turn out onto a wire rack to cool completely.

For the filling, whisk together the icing/confectioners' sugar, cocoa powder, butter and cream cheese until you have a smooth, thick icing, adding a little milk if the mixture is too stiff.

For the ganache, put the cream, chocolate, butter and syrup in a heatproof bowl set over a pan of simmering water, making sure that the bottom of the bowl does not touch the water. Heat until the chocolate has melted, then stir everything together so that you have a smooth glossy sauce.

Place one of the cakes on a serving plate and use a palette knife or metal spatula to spread over a thick layer of buttercream filling. Place the second cake on top and spread with a thick layer of the ganache. Place the bird in the centre and leave the ganache to set before serving.

This cake will keep for up to 2 days stored in an airtight container, although it is best eaten on the day it is made.

Yogurt Bundt cake with fresh berries

This is such a simple cake, just plain old vanilla, but by using a decorative Bundt pan and dusting with icing/confectioners' sugar, the cake comes to life. The cake has extra yogurt added to the batter to make it nice and moist. Filled with fresh berries to serve with each slice of cake and whipped cream on the side, this cake is simplicity itself.

200 g/scant 1 cup Greek/ US strained plain yogurt

½ teaspoon vanilla bean powder or 1 teaspoon pure vanilla extract

1 recipe 5-egg Cake Batter (see page 9)

icing/confectioners' sugar, for dusting

fresh berries and fruit, to serve

double/heavy cream, whipped to stiff peaks, or crème fraîche, to serve

a 25-cm/10-inch Bundt pan, greased

Serves 10

Preheat the oven to 180°C (350°F) Gas 4.

Fold the yogurt and vanilla into the cake batter using a spatula and spoon into the prepared Bundt pan. Bake in the preheated oven for 40–50 minutes until the cake springs back to the touch and a knife inserted into the centre of the cake comes out clean. Let cool in the pan. To remove once cooled, slide a knife around the edges of the pan to loosen the cake and then invert it onto a cake stand or plate.

Place the cake on a cake stand and dust liberally with icing/ confectioners' sugar. Fill the centre of the cake with fresh berries and fruit and serve with spoonfuls of whipped cream.

This cake will store for up to 2 days in an airtight container, but should only be topped with fruit just before serving.

Glazed apricot cake

When apricots are ripe and in season, there are few nicer cakes than this one. Topped with glazed poached apricots and with a filling of apricots roasted in Madeira, this cake tastes of pure summertime.

½ teaspoon vanilla powder or 1 teaspoon pure vanilla extract

1 recipe 4-egg Cake Batter (see page 9)

1 tablespoon apricot jam/jelly

1 packet of fixing gel or 2 tablespoons apricot glaze

300 ml/1¼ cups double/heavy cream

food-safe, pesticide-free flowers, such as Graham Thomas roses, to decorate

FOR THE APRICOTS

750 g/1 lb 10 oz. apricots

150 g/¾ cup caster/granulated sugar

250 ml/1 cup Madeira wine

50 g/3½ tablespoons butter

2 x 20-cm/8-inch round cake pans, greased and lined with baking parchment

Serves 10

Start by preparing the apricots. Put half of the apricots, whole, in a saucepan with 1 litre/4 cups water, 100 g/½ cup of the sugar and 125 ml/½ cup of the Madeira wine. Simmer for about 5 minutes until the fruit is just soft. Strain the fruit and leave to cool.

Preheat the oven to 180°C (350°F) Gas 4.

Cut the remaining apricots in half and remove the stones/pits. Put them in a roasting pan and drizzle with the remaining Madeira wine, sprinkle with the remaining sugar and dot with the butter. Bake in the preheated oven for about 20 minutes, until the fruit is soft and the juice is syrupy. Set aside to cool. Leave the oven on for the cake.

Fold the vanilla into the cake batter and divide the mixture equally between the two prepared cake pans. Bake for 25–30 minutes, until the cakes are golden brown and spring back to the touch and a knife inserted into the centre of each cake comes out clean. Let cool in the pans for a few minutes, then turn out onto a wire rack to cool completely.

When you are ready to serve, brush the top of one of the cakes with the apricot jam. This will prevent the cake from becoming soggy when the poached apricots are placed on top. Cut the poached apricots in half, remove the stones/pits and arrange in a decorative pattern on top of the cake. Make up the fixing gel according to the packet instructions, adding a tablespoon of the roasting liquid from the apricots to flavour the gel. Carefully pour over the apricot topped cake and leave to set. (If you are using the apricot glaze in place of the gel, heat gently in a saucepan with a tablespoon of the poaching liquor and brush over the tops of the apricots using a pastry brush.)

Reserve two-thirds of the roasted apricots and purée the remaining one-third with the cooking juices in a food processor. Put the cream in a large bowl and whisk to stiff peaks. Stir through the apricot purée to achieve a rippled effect. Spread the apricot cream in swirls over the top of the other cake and top with the reserved roasted apricots. Put the decorated, glazed cake on top. Decorate with flowers, if you wish, but remove them as you cut the cake. Never eat floral decorations unless you are certain it is safe to do so.

Serve straight away or store in the refrigerator until you are ready to serve. As the cake contains fresh cream, it is best eaten on the day it is made, although it will keep for up to 2 days in the refrigerator.

Naked carrot cake squares

Carrot cake is one of the most popular cakes for an afternoon teatime treat. Decorated simply with cinnamon candied carrots, this cake is rustic and delicious.

200 ml/¾ cup vegetable oil

3 eggs

250 g/1¼ cups caster/granulated sugar

70 g/⅓ cup soft dark brown sugar

150 ml/⅔ cup sour cream

250 g/generous 1¾ cups self-raising/self-rising flour, sifted

100 g/1 cup ground almonds

1 teaspoon ground cinnamon

1 teaspoon ground ginger

½ teaspoon vanilla bean powder

1 teaspoon ground mixed spice/apple pie spice

a pinch of ground nutmeg

200 g/scant 3 cups soft long shredded sweetened coconut

60 g/½ cup roasted chopped hazelnuts

300 g/10½ oz. carrots, grated

100 ml/⅓ cup orange juice

grated zest of 1 lemon

FOR THE CARROTS

3 carrots

100 g/½ cup caster/granulated sugar, plus extra for sprinkling

freshly squeezed juice of 1 lemon

½ cinnamon stick

1 teaspoon pure vanilla extract

carrot top leaves, to decorate

FOR THE FROSTING

1 tablespoon cream cheese

300 g/generous 2 cups icing/confectioners' sugar, sifted

1 tablespoon butter, softened

½ teaspoon ground cinnamon

freshly squeezed juice of 1 lemon

a 30 x 20-cm/12 x 8-inch cake pan, greased and lined with baking parchment

a baking sheet, lined with a silicone mat or greased

Makes 24

For the carrots, peel the carrots, then, using a sharp knife, cut them into small triangles to look like carrots. Put 400 ml/1⅔ cups of water in a saucepan with the sugar, lemon juice, cinnamon stick and vanilla, and bring the syrup to the boil so that the sugar dissolves. Add the carrots and simmer in the syrup for 2–3 minutes, until just soft. Drain the carrots and remove the cinnamon stick and discard. Spread the carrots out on a baking sheet, sprinkle with a thin layer of sugar and leave in a warm place to dry overnight.

Preheat the oven to 150°C (300°F) Gas 2.

For the cake, in a large mixing bowl whisk together the vegetable oil, eggs, caster/granulated sugar, brown sugar and sour cream. Sift in the flour and ground almonds and add the cinnamon, ginger, vanilla, mixed spice/apple pie spice and nutmeg and whisk everything together. Fold in the coconut and hazelnuts. In a separate bowl, pour the orange juice over the grated carrots, stirring well so that all the carrot is coated in the juice. Fold the carrot and orange juice and lemon zest into the cake batter. Pour the mixture into the prepared pan and bake in the preheated oven for 1¼–1½ hours, until the cake is firm to the touch, golden brown and a knife inserted into the centre of the cake comes out clean. Leave to cool in the pan.

For the frosting, whisk together the cream cheese, icing/confectioners' sugar, butter, cinnamon and lemon juice to make a thick and creamy icing. You may not need all of the lemon juice, so add it gradually. Using a palette knife or metal spatula, spread the frosting over the cake. Cut the cake into 24 squares and place a few candied carrots and a sprig of carrot top leaves on top of each cake.

These cakes will keep for up to 3 days stored in an airtight container, but it is best to decorate with the carrots just before serving.

Gluten-free ginger and vanilla cake

Although this sponge is gluten-free, you would not know it and it is therefore nice enough to serve to anyone, whether they are allergic to wheat or not. Filled with a delicate whipped ginger cream and topped with pretty camomile flowers or daisies, this is a simple summer cake. It is important to use gluten-free icing/confectioners' sugar, as some anti-caking agents contain wheat.

225 g/1 generous cup caster/granulated sugar

225 g/2 sticks butter, softened

4 eggs

140 g/generous 1⅓ cups ground almonds

115 g gluten-free self-raising flour OR generous ¾ cup gluten-free all-purpose flour plus 1 teaspoon gluten-free baking powder and ½ teaspoon xanthan gum, sifted

1 teaspoon ground ginger

½ teaspoon vanilla bean powder or 1 teaspoon pure vanilla extract

a pinch of salt

2 tablespoons buttermilk

4 balls stem ginger preserved in syrup, finely chopped, plus 1 tablespoon of the preserving syrup

icing/confectioners' sugar, for dusting

edible, pesticide-free camomile flowers or daisies, to decorate

FOR THE FILLING

250 ml/1 cup double/heavy cream

2 tablespoons ginger syrup

2 x 20-cm/8-inch round cake pans, greased and lined with baking parchment

Serves 10

Preheat the oven to 180°C (350°F) Gas 4.

For the cake, whisk together the sugar and butter until light and creamy. Whisk in the eggs one at a time, beating after each egg is added. Add the ground almonds, flour, ground ginger, vanilla and salt and whisk in. Fold in the buttermilk, chopped ginger and ginger syrup, then divide the mixture equally between the prepared cake pans. Bake in the preheated oven for 30–40 minutes, until the cakes are golden brown and spring back to the touch and a knife inserted into the centre of each cake comes out clean. Leave to cool in the pans for a few minutes, then turn out onto a wire rack to cool completely.

When you are ready to serve, put the cream and ginger syrup in a mixing bowl and whisk to stiff peaks. Place one of the cakes on your serving plate and top with large spoonfuls of the cream. Place the second cake on top and dust with icing/confectioners' sugar. Place the camomile flowers or daisies on top of the cake and serve immediately. Although the flowers are edible, they are best used for decoration purposes only, as they can have a bitter taste. Never consume floral decorations unless you are certain it is safe to do so.

Serve straight away or store in the refrigerator until you are ready to serve. As the cake contains fresh cream, it is best eaten on the day it is made, although it will keep for up to 2 days in the refrigerator, topping with the flowers just before serving for the prettiest results.

Orange and white chocolate dome cakes

These pretty little dome cakes look positively volcanic. They are bursting with orange zest and prettily decorated with white chocolate and classic chocolate-covered orange peel. If you prefer lemon, simply substitute lemon zest in the batter, use the juice of 4 lemons for the syrup and top with chocolate-coated lemon peel instead for equally delicious treats.

grated zest of 2 oranges

1 teaspoon vanilla extract

1 recipe 4-egg Cake Batter (see page 9)

FOR THE SYRUP

freshly squeezed juice of 3 oranges

2 tablespoons icing/ confectioners' sugar, sifted

FOR THE DECORATION

100 g/3½ oz. white chocolate

18 chocolate-coated orange peel sticks

3 x 6-hole chocolate teacake moulds or silicone muffin moulds, greased

Makes 18

Preheat the oven to 180°C (350°F) Gas 4.

Fold the orange zest and vanilla into the cake batter and divide between the holes of the moulds. If you only have one teacake mould, cook the cakes in batches, washing the mould between each use. Bake in the preheated oven for 20–25 minutes, until the cakes are golden brown and spring back to the touch. Press the cakes out of the moulds and cool on a wire rack. When cool, place on a rack, flat-side down, so that the cakes look dome-shaped.

For the syrup, in a saucepan, heat the orange juice and icing/ confectioners' sugar and bring to the boil. Remove from the heat and, using a large spoon, drizzle over the tops of the cakes. It is best to place a sheet of foil under the rack to catch any drips.

To make the decoration, put the white chocolate in a heatproof bowl set over a pan of simmering water, making sure that the bottom of the bowl does not touch the water. Heat until melted, stirring so that the chocolate is smooth. Let cool.

Using a teaspoon, drizzle chocolate onto the top of each cake. Place a chocolate orange stick in the centre of each and leave for the chocolate to set.

These cakes will keep for up to 2 days stored in an airtight container, although they are best eaten on the day they are made.

Dramatic Effect

Cherry and almond cakes with chocolate-dipped cherries

I love the combination of chocolate and cherries – rich and indulgent. These cakes are perfect when cherries are in season, but if you cannot get fresh cherries you could top with a glacé cherry instead.

340 g/3 sticks butter, softened

340 g/1¾ cups caster/granulated sugar

6 eggs

225 g/2¼ cups ground almonds

140 g/1 generous cup self-raising/self-rising flour, sifted

1 teaspoon almond extract

50 g/⅔ cup flaked/slivered almonds

FOR THE CHOCOLATE ICING

100 g/3½ oz. plain/bittersweet chocolate, melted

250 g/1¾ cups fondant icing/confectioners' sugar, sifted

2 tablespoons golden syrup/light corn syrup

1–2 tablespoons water (optional)

FOR THE DECORATION

about 20 fresh cherries

50 g/2 oz. white chocolate, melted

a 38 x 28-cm/15 x 11-inch rectangular baking pan, greased and lined with baking parchment

a 7-cm/3-inch round cutter (optional)

Makes about 20

Preheat the oven to 180°C (350°F) Gas 4.

For the cake, cream together the butter and sugar in a large mixing bowl. Add the eggs, one at a time, whisking after each egg is added. Add the ground almonds, flour and almond extract, and fold in gently using a spatula. Spoon the mixture into the prepared cake pan and sprinkle with the flaked/slivered almonds. Bake in the preheated oven for 25–30 minutes, until the cake is golden brown and springs back to the touch and a knife inserted into the centre of the cake comes out clean. Leave to cool in the pan, then turn out of the pan and cut the cake into about 20 rounds using the cutter.

For the icing, gently heat the chocolate, icing/confectioners' sugar and syrup in a saucepan and beat together, adding 1–2 tablespoons of water if the mixture is too thick. Spoon a little of the icing over each cake, allowing it to drizzle down the sides a little.

Half-dip the cherries in the melted white chocolate and place them on top of the cakes. Leave the icing and chocolate to set before serving.

These cakes will keep for up to 3 days stored in an airtight container.

Chequerboard cake

For best results you need a chequerboard or checkerboard pan to make this cake as this gives the correct sized rings of each cake batter to ensure that you have a perfect checked effect. If you do not have a chequerboard pan set, you can achieve a similar effect by piping alternating rings of cake batter into three sandwich pans, taking care that the rings of batter are the same diameter so that when the layers are placed together they form a chequerboard/checkerboard pattern.

1 recipe 6-egg Cake Batter
(see page 9)

60 g/scant ⅔ cup unsweetened
cocoa powder, sifted

a pinch of vanilla salt
(or a pinch of sea salt and
1 teaspoon pure vanilla extract)

100 g/3½ oz. white chocolate,
melted and cooled

4 tablespoons cherry jam/jelly

FOR THE ICING

250 g/1¾ cups icing/
confectioners' sugar, sifted,
plus extra for dusting

50 g/3½ tablespoons butter,
softened

60 g/2 oz. white chocolate,
melted and cooled

1 tablespoon milk (if needed)

*3 x 20-cm/8-inch chequerboard/
checkerboard pan sets with ring
insert, greased and lined with
baking parchment*

*2 piping/pastry bags fitted with
large round nozzles/tips*

Serves 10

Preheat the oven to 180°C (350°F) Gas 4.

Divide the cake batter almost in half with slightly more batter in one bowl (as there are 5 rings of dark chocolate cake and 4 rings of white chocolate cake). Fold the cocoa powder and a little vanilla salt into the bowl with the larger quantity of batter. Fold the melted white chocolate and a little more vanilla salt into the smaller portion of batter. Spoon each batter into a piping/pastry bag. Using the chequerboard ring insert, pipe rings of the batter in alternating colours into each prepared cake pan. Remove the chequerboard ring and tap each pan on the worktop once the inserts are removed so that there are no gaps between the cake batters. Bake for 25–30 minutes until the cakes spring back to the touch and a knife inserted into the centre of each cake comes out clean. Leave to cool in the pans for a few minutes, then turn out onto a wire rack to cool completely.

For the frosting, whisk together the icing/confectioners' sugar, butter and cooled melted white chocolate until you have a smooth, stiff icing, adding a little milk if the mixture is too stiff.

Place one of the cakes with an outer dark chocolate ring on your serving plate and spread over half of the buttercream and then half of the jam. Top with the cake that has the white chocolate outer ring and spread with the remaining buttercream and jam. Finish with the remaining cake.

Dust with icing/confectioners' sugar to serve.

This cake will keep for up to 2 days stored in an airtight container.

Passion fruit and chocolate layer cake

Chocolate and passion fruit are a quirky combination – the bitterness of the chocolate enhances the tanginess of the passion fruit. Topped with cape gooseberries and a passion flower, this cake is fit for a very special occasion.

juice of 5 passion fruit, seeds removed

yellow food colouring

1 recipe 5-egg Cake Batter (see page 9)

FOR THE BUTTERCREAM

170 g/1¼ cups icing/confectioners' sugar, sifted

45 g/scant ½ cup unsweetened cocoa powder, sifted

45 g/3 tablespoons butter, softened

1 tablespoon milk

FOR THE GANACHE

80ml/⅓ cup double/heavy cream

100 g/3½ oz. plain/bittersweet chocolate

1 tablespoon butter

1 tablespoon golden/light corn syrup

FOR THE DECORATION

about 15 Cape gooseberries (physalis)

food-safe, pesticide-free passion flower

2 x 20-cm/8-inch and 2 x 10-cm/4-inch round cake pans, greased and lined with baking parchment

Serves 12

Preheat the oven to 180°C (350°F) Gas 4.

Fold the passion fruit juice and a few drops of yellow food colouring into the cake batter. Spoon the mixture into the prepared cake pans, dividing approximately two-thirds of the mixture between the two larger pans and the remaining one-third of the mixture between the two smaller pans. Bake in the preheated oven for 20–30 minutes, until the cakes are golden brown and spring back to the touch and a knife inserted into the centre of each cake comes out clean. The smaller cakes will take less time to cook than the larger ones, so check them towards the end of the cooking time. Leave the cakes to cool in the pan for a few minutes, then turn out onto a wire rack to cool completely.

For the buttercream, whisk together the icing/confectioners' sugar, cocoa, butter and milk to a smooth, thick icing.

For the ganache, put the cream, chocolate, butter and syrup in a heatproof bowl set over a pan of simmering water, making sure that the bottom of the bowl does not touch the water. Heat until the chocolate has melted, then stir everything together so that you have a smooth, glossy sauce.

To assemble, place one of the larger cakes on a serving plate. Spread approximately two-thirds of the buttercream over the top of the cake using a palette knife or metal spatula. Place the second large cake on top. Spread about two-thirds of the ganache over the top of the cake. Place one of the smaller cakes in the centre of the large cakes. Spread the remaining buttercream over the top of the small cake and top with the final small cake. Cover the top cake with the remaining ganache in a thick layer.

To decorate the cake, place the Cape gooseberries around the edge of the large cake and dust with a little icing/confectioners' sugar. Place the passion flower on top. The passion flower is for decoration only and should be removed before cutting the cake. Never eat floral decorations unless you are certain it is safe to do so.

This cake will keep for up to 2 days stored in an airtight container.

Green tea ice cream cake

These pretty pink cakes are filled with trendy green tea ice cream, made with matcha powder. Topped with pretty blossom decorations, they are perfect to serve in the summer when it is warm. If you do not have time to make the ice cream, you can substitute store-bought ice cream in any flavour of your choosing.

½ teaspoon vanilla bean powder or 1 teaspoon pure vanilla extract

1 recipe 4-egg Cake Batter (see page 9)

pink food colouring

FOR THE ICE CREAM

1 teaspoon matcha green tea powder

400 ml/1¾ cups double/heavy cream

200 ml/¾ cup milk

5 egg yolks

100 g/½ cup caster/granulated sugar

green food colouring (optional)

TO DECORATE

icing/confectioners' sugar, for dusting

50 g/2 oz. plain/bittersweet chocolate, melted and cooled

sugar flowers

an ice cream maker (optional)

2 x 20-cm/8-inch round cake pans, greased and lined with baking parchment

a piping/pastry bag fitted with small round nozzle/tip

a 6.5-cm/2½-inch round cutter

Serves 10

Begin by preparing the ice cream. Heat the green tea powder with the cream and milk in a saucepan over medium heat and bring to the boil, whisking all the time so that the powder dissolves. In a mixing bowl, whisk together the egg yolks and sugar until very thick and creamy and pale yellow in colour. Bring the cream to the boil again and pour over the eggs in a thin stream, whisking all the time. Return to the pan and cook for a few minutes further until the mixture begins to thicken, stirring all the time. Add a few drops of green food colouring if you want a more vibrant colour. Pour the mixture into a the bowl and leave to cool completely. Churn in an ice cream maker following manufacturer's instructions and store in the freezer until you are ready to serve. If you do not have an ice cream maker, pour the mixture into a freezer-proof box and put in the freezer, whisking every 20 minutes or so until frozen to break up the ice crystals.

Preheat the oven to 180°C (350°F) Gas 4.

Fold the vanilla into the cake batter, add a few drops of pink food colouring and fold in gently until you have an even colour. Divide the mixture equally between the prepared cake pans. Bake in the preheated oven for 20–30 minutes, until the cakes spring back to the touch and a knife inserted into the centre of each cake comes out clean. Leave to cool in the pans for a few minutes, then turn out onto a wire rack to cool completely.

Once cool, cut out 5 circles of sponge from each cake using the cutter. (The trimmings are not needed for the recipe, but you can blitz these to make cake crumbs and store in the freezer for another recipe that needs them, such as truffles or cake pops.) Cut each circle of cake in half horizontally. Dust the top half of each cake with icing/confectioners' sugar, then spoon the melted chocolate into the piping/pastry bag. Pipe lines of chocolate onto the cake tops to make a branch pattern and decorate with the sugar flowers. Leave to set before serving.

Shortly before you are ready to serve, remove the ice cream from the freezer and allow to soften slightly. Using the same cutter, cut out 10 rounds of ice cream. Use a knife to slice under the cutter and remove from your ice cream block. Sandwich each ice cream round between two cake halves with the decorated cake half on top. Serve immediately.

White chocolate, peppermint and vanilla layer cake

I love the refreshing combination of vanilla and mint. With gradating pale green cake layers, creamy white chocolate frosting and delicate crystallized mint leaves, this cake is too tempting to resist.

½ teaspoon vanilla bean powder or 1 teaspoon pure vanilla extract

a pinch of regular salt

1 recipe 6-egg Cake Batter (see page 9)

green food colouring gel

FOR THE WHITE CHOCOLATE BUTTERCREAM

350 g/2½ cups icing/confectioners' sugar, sifted

1 tablespoon butter, softened

100 g/3½ oz. white chocolate, melted and cooled

1 teaspoon peppermint extract

a little milk (if needed)

FOR THE FROSTED MINT LEAVES

1 egg white

fresh mint leaves

caster/superfine sugar, for sprinkling

a paint brush

a baking sheet, lined with a silicone mat or baking parchment

4 x 20-cm/8-inch round cake pans, greased and lined with baking parchment

Serves 10

Begin by preparing the frosted mint leaves as they need to dry overnight. Whisk the egg white until very foamy. Using a paint brush, paint the egg white on both the front and the back of each leaf and sprinkle with sugar so that each leaf is coated in a thin layer. Place on the silicone mat or prepared baking sheet. Leave in a warm place to dry overnight. Once dried, store in an airtight container until needed.

Preheat the oven to 180°C (350°F) Gas 4.

Fold the vanilla and salt into the cake batter using a spatula. Add a drop of food colouring gel to the batter and whisk in. Spoon a quarter of the mixture into one of the prepared cake pans. Add another few drops of food colouring to the remaining batter and whisk in to make a slightly darker green colour. Spoon a third of the batter into another of the cake pans. Repeat with the remaining two portions of batter, adding a little more colouring each time until you have 4 cakes of varying shades of green. Bake in the preheated oven for 25–30 minutes, until the cakes spring back to the touch and a knife inserted into the centre of each cake comes out clean. Leave to cool in the pans for a few minutes, then turn out onto a wire rack to cool completely.

For the white chocolate buttercream, whisk together the icing/confectioners' sugar, butter, melted chocolate and peppermint extract until you have a smooth, thick icing, adding a little milk if the mixture is too stiff.

Using a large, serrated knife, trim away the edges of the cake to reveal the different colours of green cake sponge. Place the darkest green cake on a cake stand or serving plate and spread over a thin layer of the buttercream. Place the next darkest cake on top and spread with more buttercream. Repeat with the remaining two layers so that you end with the lightest-coloured green cake on top. Spread a layer of buttercream over the top of the cake and decorate with the crystallized mint leaves.

This cake will keep for up to 3 days stored in an airtight container.

Coffee and pineapple layer cake

Coffee and pineapple may seem an unusual combination but are utterly delicious together. This cake is decorated with crisp pineapple flowers and is topped with a delicious mascarpone icing. You need to prepare the pineapple crisps the day before, as they need to dry overnight.

1 pineapple

1 shot espresso coffee

1 teaspoon coffee extract

½ teaspoon coffee salt (optional)

1 recipe 4-egg Cake Batter (see page 9)

FOR THE COFFEE SYRUP

1 shot espresso

1 tablespoon caster/ granulated sugar

FOR THE MASCARPONE CREAM

170 g/6 oz. mascarpone cheese

60 g/4 tablespoons butter, softened

450 g/3¼ cups icing/ confectioners' sugar, sifted

2 x 20-cm/8-inch round cake pans, greased and lined with baking parchment

a baking sheet, lined with a silicone mat or baking parchment

Serves 10

Peel the pineapple and slice it in half across the middle. Reserve one half of the pineapple for the filling (store wrapped in clingfilm/plastic wrap in the refrigerator until you are ready to assemble the cake). Cut the other half into very thin rounds using a very sharp knife. Place the slices on the prepared baking sheet and leave in a warm place to dry overnight. Alternatively, you can dry the pineapple slices in your oven set on the lowest possible setting, checking them every hour. The length of time they will need to dry will depend on the heat of your oven and the ripeness of your pineapple.

Preheat the oven to 180°C (350°F) Gas 4.

Fold the espresso, coffee extract and coffee salt into the cake batter and divide the mixture equally between the prepared cake pans. Bake in the preheated oven for 20–30 minutes, until the cakes are golden brown and spring back to the touch and a knife inserted into the centre of each cake comes out clean. Leave to cool in the pans for a few minutes, then turn out onto a wire rack to cool completely.

For the coffee syrup, heat the espresso and sugar in a saucepan until the sugar has dissolved and the mixture is syrupy. Leave to cool.

For the mascarpone cream filling, whisk together the mascarpone cheese, butter and icing/confectioners' sugar until you have a smooth, thick icing.

Core the reserved pineapple half and cut into thin slices. Cut both cakes in half horizontally using a sharp knife so that you have four layers of cake. Place one cake half on a serving plate and drizzle with a little of the coffee syrup. Cover with a layer of pineapple slices, then place a second cake half on top. Spread over half of the mascarpone cream, then top with another cake half. Drizzle the sponge with a little of the coffee syrup and more pineapple slices. Top with the final cake half and drizzle the top and sides of the cake with a little of the coffee syrup. Cover the top of the cake with the remaining mascarpone cream and decorate with the dried pineapple crisps.

It is best to assemble the cake just before serving, but this cake will keep for up to 2 days stored in an airtight container.

Redcurrant cake

On family holidays to Alsace in France, I remember making redcurrant tarts. I love the sharpness of these tangy red berries. These little cakes are filled with redcurrant compôte and are topped with delicious custard and cream.

280 g/scant 1 cup caster/
granulated sugar

280 g/2½ sticks butter, softened

5 eggs

280 g/generous 2 cups
self-raising/self-rising
flour, sifted

80 ml/⅓ cup buttermilk

1 teaspoon pure vanilla extract

FOR THE COMPÔTE

300 g/3 cups redcurrants

60 g/generous ¼ cup caster/
granulated sugar

FOR THE CRÈME PATISSIÈRE

1 egg and 1 egg yolk

2 tablespoons cornflour/
cornstarch, sifted

80 g/⅓ cup plus 1 tablespoon
caster/granulated sugar

250 ml/1 cup double/heavy
cream

1 teaspoon vanilla powder
or pure vanilla extract

TO DECORATE

icing/confectioners' sugar,
for dusting

200 ml/generous ¾ cup
double/heavy cream

*6 x 8-cm/3-inch raised-centre
flan pans, greased*

Makes 6

Preheat the oven to 180°C (350°F) Gas 4.

For the cake, whisk together the sugar and butter in a large mixing bowl until light and creamy. Whisk in the eggs one at a time. Fold in the flour, buttermilk and vanilla, and spoon the mixture into the prepared flan pans. Bake in the preheated oven for 20–30 minutes, until the cakes spring back to the touch and a knife inserted into one of the cake comes out clean. Leave to cool in the pan for a few minutes, then turn out onto a wire rack to cool completely.

To prepare the compôte, put the redcurrants, sugar and 2 tablespoons water in an ovenproof dish and bake at the same time as the cake for 20–30 minutes, until the fruit is soft. Remove from the oven and leave to cool.

For the crème patissière, whisk the egg and egg yolk, cornflour/cornstarch and sugar together in a large heatproof bowl until very thick and creamy. In a saucepan, bring the cream and vanilla to the boil. Whisking all the time, pour the hot cream over the egg mixture. Return the mixture to the saucepan and whisk continuously until the custard thickens. Take care that the mixture does not start to curdle. If it does, pass the mixture through a sieve/strainer to remove any lumps, pressing it through with the back of a spoon. Leave to cool.

Place the cakes on serving plates and spread the melted chocolate into the cavities. Dust the whole cakes with a good layer of icing/confectioners' sugar. Spoon the compôte on top of the chocolate and cover with the custard.

Whip the cream to stiff peaks and spoon over the custard in swirled peaks. Decorate with the fresh redcurrants.

Serve straight away or store in the refrigerator until you are ready to serve. As the cakes contains fresh cream, they are best eaten on the day they are made, although they will keep for up to 2 days in the refrigerator.

Chocolate fig cake

This cake is a fig lover's delight, with roasted figs decorating the cake. Rich with cocoa powder, and sandwiched with zingy cream cheese frosting, this naked cake will have a dramatic effect in the centre of any party table.

60 g/generous ½ cup unsweetened cocoa powder, sifted

1 recipe 6-egg Cake Batter (see page 9)

4 tablespoons lemon curd

FOR THE BAKED FIGS

6 figs

1 tablespoon caster/ superfine sugar

1 tablespoon runny honey

a knob of butter

FOR THE BUTTERCREAM

350 g/2½ cups icing/ confectioners' sugar, sifted

1 tablespoon butter, softened

1 tablespoon cream cheese

a little milk (if needed)

TO DECORATE

50 g/2 oz. white chocolate, melted

icing/confectioners' sugar, for dusting

3 x 20-cm/8-inch round cake pans, greased and lined with baking parchment

a silicone mat or greased baking sheet

Serves 10

Preheat the oven to 180°C (350°F) Gas 4.

Put the figs in a roasting pan and sprinkle over the sugar. Drizzle over the honey and dot each fig with a little butter. Bake in the preheated oven for 15–20 minutes, until the figs are soft but still retain their shape. Let cool, but leave the oven on to cook the cake.

Fold the cocoa powder into the cake batter and divide the mixture equally between the prepared cake pans. Bake in the preheated oven for 20–30 minutes, until the cakes spring back to the touch and a knife inserted into the centre of each cake comes out clean. Let cool in the pans for a few minutes, then turn out onto a wire rack to cool completely.

For the buttercream, whisk together the icing/confectioners' sugar, butter and cream cheese until you have a smooth, stiff icing, adding a little milk if the mixture is too stiff.

Using a large serrated knife, cut each cake in half horizontally. Place one half on a serving plate or cake stand and spread with a little of the buttercream. Spoon over some of the lemon curd and top with a second cake half. Repeat with the remaining cakes. Spread the remaining buttercream thinly around the edge of the cake, so that you can still just see the layers. Dust with icing/confectioners' sugar and drizzle the top with white chocolate in pretty patterns.

To decorate, cut the baked figs in half and arrange on top and around the base of the cake. Serve straight away. The cake will store for up to 2 days in an airtight container, but only decorate with the figs just before serving.

Croquembouche

This is perhaps the original naked cake, where the decoration is really from the stunning mound of profiteroles themselves rather than any fancy icing.

FOR THE CHOUX PASTRY

260 g/2 cups plain/all-purpose flour, sifted twice

200 g/1¾ sticks butter, cut into cubes

a pinch of salt

8 eggs

FOR THE FILLING

600 ml/2½ cups double/heavy cream

2 tablespoons icing/confectioners' sugar

1 teaspoon vanilla bean powder or 2 teaspoons pure vanilla extract

TO ASSEMBLE AND DECORATE

600 g/2 cups caster/granulated sugar

food-safe flowers, such as jasmine flowers, to decorate

4 baking sheets, lined with baking parchment or silicone mats (or rewash and dry between use)

2 piping/pastry bags fitted with round nozzles/tips

a large sheet of thin cardboard

sellotape

Serves 20–30

Heat the butter in a large saucepan with 600 ml/2½ cups of water and the salt until the butter is melted. As soon as the butter is melted, quickly add the sifted flour all in one go and remove the pan from the heat. Do not let the water boil for longer than it takes to melt the butter, as it will evaporate. Beat the mixture very hard with a wooden spoon until it forms a ball and no longer sticks to the sides of the pan. At first the mixture will seem very wet, but it will come together after a few minutes. It is important to beat the mixture well at this stage. Let cool for 5 minutes.

In a separate bowl, whisk the eggs, then beat them into the pastry dough, a small amount at a time, using a wooden spoon or a balloon whisk. The mixture will split slightly at first, but this is normal and the dough will come back together as you continue to beat. Beat the mixture very hard at each stage. The mixture will form a sticky paste that holds its shape when you lift the whisk up. (You may prefer to make the choux pastry in 2 batches, as it is easier to beat this way.)

Preheat the oven to 200°C (400°F) Gas 6. Spoon the choux pastry into the piping/pastry bag and pipe about 80 small balls of pastry onto the baking sheets. Using a clean, wet finger, smooth down any peaks. Sprinkle a little water into the bottom of the oven to create steam. Bake the first baking sheet of profiteroles for 10 minutes, then reduce the oven to 180°C (350°F) Gas 4 and bake for 10–15 minutes more until crisp. Cut a slit into each profiterole to allow any steam to escape, then let cool on a wire rack. Repeat with the remaining sheets. (You can cook the sheets at the same time, but the lower choux will take longer to cook.) Once cool, make a small hole in the base of each profiterole using a sharp knife.

For the filling, whisk together the cream, icing/confectioners' sugar and vanilla to stiff peaks, then spoon into the second piping/pastry bag. Pipe a small amount of cream into each of the profiteroles.

Make a cone with the cardboard, trimming the base so it stands flat, approximately 40 cm/16 inches high and 18 cm/7 inches in diameter across the base, securing in place with sellotape. Place on a cake stand.

In a saucepan set over medium heat, heat the sugar until melted. It is best to do this in two saucepans, heating half the sugar in each. Do not stir, but swirl the pan to ensure that the sugar does not burn. Once the sugar has melted, carefully dip each bun into the caramel using tongs. Place the dipped profiteroles in a ring around the base of the cone. Repeat with all the remaining profiteroles and build them up around the cone. Reheat the sugar if it becomes to solid. Once the tower is assembled, dip a fork into the remaining sugar and then spin it over the tower of profiteroles in thin lines.

Serve at once, as the spun sugar will soften over time.

Chocolate Guinness cake

The Guinness in this cake really enhances the flavour of the chocolate, giving it a savoury bitterness that is a perfect counterfoil for the sweet icing. With lots of cocoa, melted chocolate and chocolate chips in the cake batter, this cake is perfect for any party or birthday celebration.

250 g/2¼ sticks butter, softened

250 g/1¼ cups soft dark brown sugar

½ teaspoon vanilla bean powder or 1 teaspoon pure vanilla extract

2 eggs

100 g/3½ oz. plain/bittersweet chocolate, melted

280 g/generous 2 cups self-raising/self-rising flour, sifted

50 g/½ cup unsweetened cocoa powder, sifted, plus extra for dusting

250 ml/1 cup Guinness or stout

150 ml/⅔ cup sour cream

100 g/⅔ cup white chocolate chips

FOR THE FROSTING

300 g/2 generous cups icing/confectioners' sugar, sifted

1 tablespoon butter, softened

2 tablespoons mascarpone cheese

a little milk (if needed)

a 25-cm/10-inch ring Bundt pan, greased

Serves 10

Preheat the oven to 180°C (350°F) Gas 4.

In a large mixing bowl, cream together the butter and dark brown sugar. Add the vanilla and eggs and whisk again. Add the melted chocolate, flour, cocoa, Guinness and sour cream and whisk until everything is incorporated. Stir through the chocolate chips and spoon the mixture into the prepared Bundt pan. Bake for 30–40 minutes, until the cake springs back to the touch and a knife inserted into the centre of the cake comes out clean. Allow the cake to cool completely in the pan, then turn out onto a wire rack, using a knife to help ease it away from the pan.

For the frosting, whisk together the icing/confectioners' sugar, butter and mascarpone cheese until you have a smooth, thick icing, adding a little milk if the frosting is too stiff.

Place the cake on a serving plate and spread the icing over the top of the cake. Dust with a little cocoa.

This cake will keep for up to 2 days stored in an airtight container.

The Changing Seasons

Lemon and lavender cakes

These pretty little cakes look so cute with gradated purple sponges and lavender sugar flowers. The cakes are filled with a delicious cream cheese buttercream and lavender lemon curd and are the perfect addition to any summertime tea party.

grated zest of 3 lemons

1 recipe 6-egg Cake Batter
(see page 9)

purple food colouring gel

icing/confectioners' sugar,
for dusting

FOR THE LAVENDER

10 sprigs of edible lavender

1 egg white

caster/superfine sugar

FOR THE DRIZZLE AND CURD

freshly squeezed juice
of 5 lemons

1 teaspoon edible lavender

2 tablespoons icing/
confectioners' sugar

3 tablespoons lemon curd

FOR THE BUTTERCREAM

350 g/2½ cups icing/
confectioners' sugar, sifted

1 tablespoon cream cheese

15 g/1 tablespoon butter,
softened

freshly squeezed juice
of 1 lemon

a paintbrush

*a baking sheet, lined with a
silicone mat or baking parchment*

*3 x 20-cm/8-inch round cake
pans, greased and lined with
baking parchment*

6½-cm/2½-inch cutter

*a piping/pastry bag fitted
with small round nozzle/tip*

Makes 10

Begin by preparing the lavender flowers, as they need to dry overnight. Whisk the egg white until very foamy. Using a paintbrush, brush the flower sprigs with egg white, then sprinkle with sugar. Repeat with all the flowers, one at a time, and place on the prepared baking sheet. Leave in a warm place to dry overnight. Once dried, store in an airtight container until needed.

Preheat the oven to 180°C (350°F) Gas 4.

Fold the lemon zest into the cake batter. Spoon one-third of the mixture into one of the prepared cake pans. Add a few drops of food colouring to the cake mixture and whisk in so that you have an even pale purple colour. Spoon half of the coloured mixture into another of the cake pans. Add a few more drops of food colouring to the remaining batter to make it a darker purple colour, then spoon the mixture into the final pan. Bake for 25–30 minutes, until they are firm to the touch and a knife inserted into the centre of each cake comes out clean.

In a small saucepan set over medium heat, heat the lemon juice, lavender and icing/confectioners' sugar and bring to the boil. Mix one tablespoon of the syrup with the lemon curd and set aside, then spoon the remaining syrup over the cakes and leave to cool in the pans.

Once cool, remove the cakes from the pans. Place one of the cakes on a chopping board and cut out 5 circles of sponge with the cutter. Discard the trimmings (these can be crumbed and frozen for use in another recipe that calls for cake crumbs, such as cake pops or truffles). Repeat with the remaining 2 cakes. Cut each small cake in half horizontally, so that you have 10 discs of cake in each colour, 30 in total.

For the buttercream, whisk together the icing/confectioners' sugar, cream cheese, butter and lemon juice until you have a smooth, stiff icing.

Spoon the buttercream into the piping/pastry bag and pipe a ring of buttercream around the edge of the 10 darkest purple cakes. Spoon a teaspoonful of the lavender lemon curd into the centre of each ring, then top each with one of the light purple-coloured cakes. Repeat with another ring of buttercream and fill with lemon curd, then top each cake with one of the plain sponges. Dust the cakes with icing/confectioners' sugar, then decorate with crystallized lavender flowers. The stalks of the lavender are not edible, so these should be removed before eating.

These cakes will keep for up to 3 days stored in an airtight container, but are best eaten on the day they are made.

Ginger cake with mascarpone and marigolds

Marigolds have such vibrant petals that make any cake look very pretty. This is a light ginger cake, rather than a heavy traditional gingerbread. Served with a little mascarpone frosting and with grated carrot and stem ginger in the cake batter, this is a rustic but delicious cake.

2 teaspoons ground ginger

6 balls stem ginger preserved in syrup, plus 3 tablespoons of the syrup

3 large carrots, peeled and grated

1 recipe 6-egg Cake Batter (see page 9)

icing/confectioners' sugar, for dusting

food-safe, pesticide-free marigold flowers, to decorate

FOR THE MASCARPONE CREAM

125 g/generous ½ cup mascarpone cheese

450 g/3¼ cups icing/confectioners' sugar, sifted

50 g/3½ tablespoons butter, softened

3–4 tablespoons milk

20-cm/8-inch and 25-cm/10-inch square loose-bottomed cake pans, greased and lined with baking parchment

a piping/pastry bag fitted with large round nozzle/tip

Serves 18

Preheat the oven to 180°C (350°F) Gas 4.

Fold the ground ginger, stem ginger and syrup, and grated carrot into the cake batter. Spoon into the prepared cake pans, dividing approximately two-thirds into the larger pan and the remaining one-third into the smaller pan so that the depth of the cakes is equal. Bake for 30–40 minutes, until the cakes are golden brown and spring back to the touch and a knife comes out clean when inserted into the centre of each cake. The smaller cake will take less time to cook than the larger one, so check regularly towards the end of the cooking time. Leave to cool in the pans for a few minutes, then turn out onto a wire rack to cool completely.

For the mascarpone cream, whisk together the mascarpone cheese, icing/confectioners' sugar, butter and milk in a large mixing bowl, adding the milk gradually as you may not need it all. You need a smooth thick icing that holds a peak when you lift up the beaters. Spoon the mascarpone cream into the piping/pastry bag.

To assemble, cut each of the cakes in half with a large serrated knife. Place the bottom half of the larger cake on a serving plate and pipe the icing around the edge of the cake. Spread some more icing over the middle of the cake so that it is covered in a thin layer of cream inside the piped lines. Top with the other half of the large cake and dust with icing/confectioners' sugar. Spread a little icing in the middle of the cake and place the bottom half of the small cake on the icing. Repeat the piping, top with the other small cake half, and dust with icing/confectioners' sugar again.

Decorate the cake with food-safe, fresh marigolds. You can eat the petals (provided that they have not been sprayed with pesticide), but do not eat the stems or any green parts. Remove the flowers before you cut the cake. Never eat floral decorations unless you are certain it is safe to do so.

This cake will keep for up to 3 days stored in an airtight container, although is best eaten on the day it is made.

Rhubarb and custard cake

Rhubarb and custard sweets were a childhood favourite of mine and this cake takes its inspiration from them. Filled with a creamy custard and poached rhubarb, and decorated very simply with pretty pink rhubarb tuiles, this cake is sure to tempt you.

½ teaspoon vanilla bean paste or 1 teaspoon vanilla extract

1 recipe 4-egg Cake Batter (see page 9)

icing/confectioners' sugar, for dusting

FOR THE ROASTED RHUBARB

600 g/21 oz. rhubarb (ideally pink), trimmed and chopped into 3-cm/1¼-inch pieces

80 g/⅓ cup plus 1 tablespoon caster/granulated sugar

1 teaspoon vanilla bean powder

FOR THE RHUBARB TUILES

2 sticks rhubarb

pink food colouring

freshly squeezed juice of 1 lemon

1 tablespoon caster/granulated sugar

FOR THE CUSTARD CREAM

200 ml/¾ cup double/heavy cream

3 tablespoons ready-made custard

1 teaspoon vanilla bean powder

a swivel vegetable peeler

a baking sheet lined with a silicone mat or baking parchment

2 x 20-cm/8-inch round cake pans, greased and lined with baking parchment

Serves 10

Begin by preparing the rhubarb tuiles as they need to dry overnight. Trim the ends of the rhubarb and peel into long thin strips using the swivel peeler. Place the strips of rhubarb in a large pan with just enough water to cover them and add a few drops of pink food colouring, the lemon juice and sugar. Simmer for 2–3 minutes until the rhubarb is just soft. Place the strips of rhubarb on the prepared baking sheet and twist into pretty shapes. Leave in a warm place to dry overnight, by which time the rhubarb should be crisp. The rhubarb is fragile so, once dried, store carefully in an airtight container until you are ready to serve.

For the roasted rhubarb, preheat the oven to 180°C (350°F) Gas 4. Put the rhubarb in an ovenproof dish with the sugar, 1 tablespoon water and the vanilla. Bake for 20–25 minutes, until the rhubarb is just soft. Let cool. Leave the oven on to bake the cake.

Fold the vanilla into the cake batter and gently fold in half of the cooled roasted rhubarb. Divide the mixture equally between the prepared cake pans. Bake for 25–30 minutes, until the cakes are golden brown and spring back to the touch and a knife inserted into the centre of each cake comes out clean. Leave to cool in the pans for a few minutes, then turn out onto a wire rack to cool completely.

For the custard filling, in a mixing bowl whisk together the cream, custard and vanilla to stiff peaks.

Place one of the cakes on a serving plate and cover with spoonfuls of the custard cream. Top with the remaining roasted rhubarb, draining it to remove any cooking liquid. Top with the second cake, dust with icing/confectioners' sugar and place the rhubarb tuiles on top.

Serve straight away or store in the refrigerator until you are ready to serve. As the cake contains fresh cream, it is best eaten on the day it is made, although it will keep for up to 2 days in the refrigerator.

Chocolate chestnut cake

Chestnut is an under-used ingredient in baking – I love its delicate flavour. This cake has layers of chestnut, chocolate and vanilla cake sandwiched together with a chestnut buttercream, and is topped with a glossy chocolate ganache and festive marrons glacés. Although marrons glacés are expensive, they are definitely worth splurging on as a treat to decorate this cake. If you prefer, you can use the slightly cheaper marron pieces rather than whole marrons glacés, for equally pretty results.

1 recipe 6-egg Cake Batter (see page 9)

40 g/generous ⅓ cup unsweetened cocoa powder, sifted

80 g/scant ¼ cup chestnut purée

1 teaspoon pure vanilla extract

10 marrons glacés

100 g/3¾ oz. plain/bittersweet chocolate, melted

FOR THE BUTTERCREAM

250 g/1¾ cups icing/confectioners' sugar, sifted

1 tablespoon butter, softened

150 g/½ cup sweetened chestnut purée

70 g/⅓ cup cream cheese

a little milk, if needed

FOR THE GANACHE

60 ml/¼ cup double/heavy cream

200 g/7 oz. plain/bittersweet chocolate

15 g/1 tablespoon butter

1 tablespoon golden syrup/light corn syrup

3 x 20-cm/8-inch round cake pans, greased and lined with baking parchment

Serves 12

Preheat the oven to 180°C (350°F) Gas 4.

Divide the cake batter equally into three bowls. Add three-quarters of the cocoa powder to one of the bowls and fold in until the cocoa is all incorporated. Add the chestnut purée and the remaining cocoa powder to another of the bowls and fold in. Add the vanilla extract to the third bowl. Spoon each cake mixture into a prepared cake pan and bake for 25–30 minutes, until the cakes spring back to the touch and a knife comes out clean when inserted into the centre of each cake. Leave to cool in the pans for a few minutes, then turn out onto a wire rack to cool completely.

For the ganache, put the cream, chocolate, butter and syrup in a heatproof bowl set over a pan of simmering water, making sure that the bottom of the bowl does not touch the water. Heat until the chocolate has melted, then stir everything together so that you have a smooth glossy sauce. Remove from the heat and leave to cool slightly.

For the buttercream, whisk together the icing/confectioners' sugar, butter, chestnut purée and cream cheese until light and creamy, adding a little milk if the mixture is too stiff.

Cut each cake in half horizontally. Layer the cakes up on a serving plate or cake stand, alternating the coloured layers (chocolate, chestnut and then vanilla, then repeating), spreading a little of the buttercream and a drizzle of chocolate ganache between each layer.

Spread the remaining ganache over the top of the cake. Dip half of the marrons glacés in the melted chocolate, then place them in a ring on top of the cake, alternating with the un-dipped marrons glacés. You need the ganache to be cooled to do this, so that it is slightly thickened and the marrons glacés do not move.

This cake will keep for up to 2 days stored in an airtight container.

Blackberry and apple cake with cinnamon buttercream

This cake is very simply decorated but looks so pretty with vibrant pink roses and glistening blackberries. The cake is flavoured with apple and is sandwiched together with delicious cinnamon buttercream and apple purée, making it a perfect cake to serve at harvest time when apples and blackberries are in season.

2 teaspoons ground cinnamon

4 dessert apples, peeled, cored and grated

1 recipe 6-egg Cake Batter (see page 9)

200 g/1½ cups blackberries

food-safe, pesticide-free pink roses, to decorate

FOR THE APPLE PURÉE

5 dessert apples

50 g/¼ cup caster/granulated sugar

15 g/1 tablespoon butter

FOR THE BUTTERCREAM

450 g/3¼ cups icing/confectioners' sugar, sifted, plus extra for dusting

100 g/7 tablespoons butter, softened

1 teaspoon ground cinnamon

3–4 tablespoons milk (if needed)

2 x 23-cm/9-inch round springform cake pans, greased and lined with baking parchment

Serves 16

Begin by preparing the apple purée, as it needs to cool before being used. Peel and core the apples and chop into small pieces. Put them in a saucepan with the sugar and 60 ml/¼ cup water and simmer over low heat until the apple is very soft. Add the butter to the pan and continue to simmer until the butter has melted, then set aside to cool.

Preheat the oven to 180°C (350°F) Gas 4.

For the cake, fold the cinnamon and grated apple into the cake batter and divide the mixture equally between the prepared cake pans. Bake for 30–40 minutes, until the cakes are golden brown and spring back to the touch and a knife inserted into the centre of each cake comes out clean. Leave to cool in the pans for a few minutes, then turn out onto a wire rack to cool completely.

For the buttercream, whisk together the icing/confectioners' sugar, butter and cinnamon until the icing is thick and creamy and holds a peak when you lift the beaters, adding a little milk if the mixture is too stiff.

To assemble the cake, use a large serrated knife to cut each cake in half horizontally. Place one of the cake halves on a serving plate or cake stand and cover with a layer of buttercream and one-third of the apple purée. Top with another cake half and repeat the layers until you have four layers of cake and all the apple purée has been used. Spread the remaining buttercream over the centre of the top of the cake and dust with a little icing/confectioners' sugar. Arrange the blackberries and roses on top of the buttercream and serve straight away. Remove the roses before you cut the cake, as they are not intended to be eaten. Never eat floral decorations unless you are confident it is safe to do so.

This cake will keep for up to 3 days stored in an airtight container, although it is best to top with the fruit and roses just before serving so that they are at their prettiest.

Pumpkin cake

This delightful cake is moist from the pumpkin purée and is delicately spiced with ginger, cinnamon and mixed spice. This is a very autumnal cake, topped with pumpkin seed sugar shards for a dramatic effect.

250 g/9 oz. pumpkin purée (such as Libby's)

½ teaspoon vanilla bean powder or 1 teaspoon pure vanilla extract

1 teaspoon ground mixed spice/apple pie spice

1 teaspoon ground ginger

1 teaspoon ground cinnamon

a pinch of ground cloves

1 recipe 6-egg Cake Batter (see page 9)

FOR THE BUTTERCREAM

350 g/2½ cups icing/ confectioners' sugar, sifted

1 tablespoon cream cheese

1 tablespoon butter, softened

a little milk (if needed)

FOR THE DECORATION

100 g/½ cup caster/superfine sugar

1 tablespoon pumpkin seeds

FOR THE GANACHE

60 ml/¼ cup double/heavy cream

200 g/7 oz. plain/bittersweet chocolate

15 g/1 tablespoon butter

1 tablespoon golden syrup/ light corn syrup

2 x 23-cm/9-inch round springform cake pans, greased and lined with baking parchment

a baking sheet, lined with a silicone mat or baking parchment

Serves 14

Preheat the oven to 180°C (350°F) Gas 4.

Fold the pumpkin purée, vanilla and ground spices into the cake batter. Divide the mixture between the prepared cake pans. Bake in the preheated oven for 30–40 minutes, until the cakes spring back to the touch and a knife comes out clean when inserted into the centre of each cake. Let cool in the pans for a few minutes, then turn out onto a wire rack to cool completely.

For the decoration, heat the sugar in a saucepan over low heat until it melts and turns light golden brown. Do not stir the pan, just swirl it to keep the sugar moving. Watch very carefully as the caramel starts to melt, as it can burn easily. Once caramelized, sprinkle the pumpkin seeds onto the prepared baking sheet and pour over the caramel. Allow to cool and set. Once set, break into shards.

For the buttercream, whisk together the icing/confectioners' sugar, cream cheese and butter until light and creamy, adding a little milk if the mixture is too stiff.

For the ganache, put the cream, chocolate, butter and syrup in a heatproof bowl set over a pan of simmering water, making sure that the bottom of the bowl does not touch the water. Heat until the chocolate has melted, then stir everything together so that you have a smooth glossy sauce. Remove from the heat and leave to cool slightly.

Place one cake on a serving plate or cake stand and spread the buttercream evenly on top using a palette knife or metal spatula. Place the second cake on top.

Spread the ganache on the top of the cake, using a palette knife or metal spatula, then decorate with the pumpkin seed shards.

This cake is best served on the day it is made, but will keep for up to 3 days stored in an airtight container. Only decorate with the sugar shards just before serving.

Hazelnut harvest cake

I love to serve this cake for Harvest Supper in our village. With sugar-work hazelnuts and a delicious hazelnut buttercream, this cake is always popular. If you prefer, you can replace the hazelnuts with pecans or walnuts for equally delicious results.

2 tablespoons hazelnut butter or hazelnut peanut butter

1 recipe 4-egg Cake Batter (see page 9)

50 g/scant ½ cup chopped roasted hazelnuts

FOR THE HAZELNUT BUTTERCREAM

1 tablespoon hazelnut butter or hazelnut spread

250 g/1¾ cups icing/confectioners' sugar, sifted

15 g/1 tablespoon butter, softened

a little milk (if needed)

FOR THE CANDIED HAZELNUTS

100 g/½ cup caster/superfine sugar

14 whole hazelnuts

an 18-cm/7-inch round loose-bottomed deep cake pan, greased and lined with baking parchment

14 wooden skewers

a baking sheet, lined with a silicone mat or baking parchment

a piping/pastry bag, fitted with a large round nozzle/tip

Serves 8

Preheat the oven to 180°C (350°F) Gas 4.

Whisk the hazelnut butter into the cake batter, then fold in the chopped roasted hazelnuts. Pour the mixture into the prepared cake pan and bake in the preheated oven for 40–50 minutes, until the cake springs back to the touch and a knife inserted into the centre of the cake comes out clean. Leave to cool in the pan for a few minutes, then turn out onto a wire rack to cool completely.

For the hazelnut buttercream, whisk together the hazelnut butter, icing/confectioners' sugar and butter until you have a smooth stiff icing, adding a little milk if the mixture is too stiff.

For the candied hazelnut decoration, heat the sugar in a saucepan over low heat until it melts and turns light golden brown. Do not stir with a spoon, just swirl the pan to keep the sugar moving. Watch very carefully as the caramel starts to melt as it can burn easily. Once caramelized, remove the pan from the heat and leave for a few minutes until the caramel just starts to thicken.

Press a skewer into each of the hazelnuts and, one by one, dip them into the caramel. Pull out of the pan so that a long strand of caramel pulls from the hazelnut. Hold the hazelnut downwards for a few seconds so that the caramel starts to set, then place on the prepared baking sheet to cool and set completely. Repeat with all the remaining hazelnuts. (It is easiest to do this with someone to help you hold the dipped hazelnuts, so that you can keep dipping whilst the caramel is still warm.) If the caramel becomes too thick, just return the pan to the heat for a few minutes. The nuts will become sticky once exposed to the air over time so it is best to prepare them shortly before you wish to serve the cake for best results.

Spoon the buttercream into the piping/pastry bag. Using a large serrated knife, cut the cake in half horizontally and place the bottom cake half on a serving plate. Pipe a layer of the hazelnut buttercream over the cake and top with the second cake half. Pipe small peaks of the buttercream over the top of the cake and decorate with a ring of the caramelized hazelnuts.

This cake will keep (without the nut decoration) for up to 3 days stored in an airtight container.

Coffee and walnut cake

I made this cake for my dad for Father's Day, as he loves coffee and walnuts. Topped with a glossy fondant coffee icing and walnut pralines, it is quick and easy to prepare and makes a perfect cake for a special celebration. Coffee salt is an amazing product and is perfect to use in this cake. It is available from good delicatessens and online.

100 g/¾ cup walnut halves or pieces

1 recipe 6-egg Cake Batter (see page 9)

1 teaspoon coffee extract

1 shot espresso coffee

a pinch of coffee salt (or regular sea salt)

500 ml/2 cups double/heavy cream

FOR THE PRALINE

100 g/½ cup caster/ superfine sugar

100 g/¾ cup walnut halves or pieces

FOR THE GLACE ICING

200 g/1½ cups fondant icing/confectioners' sugar, sifted

1 shot of espresso

1 teaspoon coffee extract

2 x 23-cm/9-inch round cake pans, greased and lined with baking parchment

a baking sheet, lined with a silicone mat or baking parchment

food processor

a piping/pastry bag fitted with large star nozzle/tip

Serves 12

Preheat the oven to 180°C (350°F) Gas 4.

Blitz the walnuts to fine crumbs in a food processor, then fold into the cake batter along with the coffee extract, espresso coffee and coffee salt, and fold in. Divide the cake mixture equally between the prepared cake pans.

Bake in the preheated oven for 25–30 minutes, until they spring back to the touch and a knife comes out clean when inserted into the centre of each cake. Let cool in the pans for a few minutes, then turn out onto a wire rack to cool completely.

For the walnut praline, heat the sugar in a saucepan over low heat until it melts, swirling the pan to prevent the sugar from burning. Do not stir. Watch very carefully as the sugar melts as it can burn very easily. Once the sugar is a golden caramel colour, spread the walnuts out on the prepared baking sheet, placing about 10 walnuts a small distance apart and the remaining nuts close together. Drizzle a little of the caramel over each of the 10 walnuts – these will be used for decoration. Pour the remaining caramel over the rest of the nuts and leave to cool, then break into shards and blitz to fine crumbs in a food processor. As the praline will be added to the cream, it is important that there are no large lumps of praline as they will not pass through the nozzle/tip of the piping/pastry bag.

For the filling, whisk the cream to stiff peaks, then fold in the praline powder using a spatula. Spoon the cream into the piping/pastry bag.

Use a serrated knife to cut the cakes in half horizontally. Place one of the cake halves on a serving plate and pipe a layer of praline cream over the cake. Top with a second cake half and pipe over stars of the cream. Repeat the cream and cake layers until all the cakes have been used.

For the icing, mix the icing/confectioners' sugar with the espresso and coffee extract until you have a smooth thick glossy icing. You may not need all of the espresso, so add it gradually. Spread the icing over the top of the cake using a palette knife or metal spatula.

Serve straight away or store in the refrigerator until you are ready to serve. As the cake contains fresh cream, it is best eaten on the day it is made, although it will keep for up to 2 days in the refrigerator.

Festive crumble Christmas cake

Christmas cake is always popular, but there are those who do not enjoy the traditional layers of marzipan and icing. This cake is especially for them, simply topped with a baked crumble topping and dusted with powdered sugar for a snow effect.

250 g/generous 1½ cups mixed fruit and peel

150 g/generous 1 cup sultanas/golden raisins

100 g/1¼ cups toasted flaked/slivered almonds

250 ml/1 cup rum

100 ml/⅓ cup Cointreau

225 g/2 sticks butter, softened

115 g/½ cup plus 1 tablespoon soft dark brown sugar

115 g/½ cup plus 1 tablespoon caster/granulated sugar

4 eggs

280 g/generous 2 cups self-raising/self-rising flour, sifted

1 teaspoon ground mixed spice/apple pie spice

1 teaspoon ground ginger

1 teaspoon ground cinnamon

FOR THE CRUMBLE TOPPING

115 g/generous ¾ cup self-raising/self-rising flour

60 g/scant ⅓ cup caster/ granulated sugar

1 teaspoon ground cinnamon

60 g/½ stick butter

icing/confectioners' sugar, for dusting

a 23-cm/9-inch round springform cake pan, greased and lined with baking parchment

food-safe festive greenery

Serves 10

Combine the mixed fruit, sultanas/golden raisins and flaked/slivered almonds in a bowl and pour over the rum and Cointreau. Cover with clingfilm/plastic wrap and leave to soak for a few hours, or overnight, until the fruit is plump.

Preheat the oven to 180°C (350°F) Gas 4.

Whisk together the butter, dark brown sugar and caster/granulated sugar in a large mixing bowl using a mixer until light and creamy. Add the eggs and whisk again. Fold in the flour, mixed spice/apple pie spice, ginger, cinnamon and the soaked fruit using a spatula until everything is incorporated. Spoon the mixture into the prepared cake pan and bake for 1 hour.

Meanwhile, prepare the crumble topping. In a large mixing bowl, mix together the flour, sugar and cinnamon and rub the butter in with your fingertips until the mixture forms large lumps. Open the oven door carefully and sprinkle over the cake and bake for 15–30 minutes more, until a knife inserted into the centre of the cake comes out clean and the crumble topping is golden brown. Leave to cool in the pan for a few minutes, then transfer to a wire rack to cool completely.

Once cooled, place the cake on a serving plate and dust the top with a good layer of icing/confectioners' sugar for a snowy effect. Position sprigs of food-safe festive greenery around the edge of the cake on the cake stand.

This cake will keep for up to 5 days stored in an airtight container.

Index

A

almonds: cherry and
      almond cakes 102
   festive crumble Christmas
      cake 140
   gluten-free ginger and
      vanilla cake 97
   macaron cake 67
   naked Battenberg 51
   naked carrot cake squares
      94
angel cake, coconut 48
apples: blackberry and apple
      cake 132
apricots: glazed apricot cake
      93
   orchard harvest sponge
      cake 79

B

banana Brazil nut caramel
      cakes 85
Battenberg, naked 51
beer: chocolate Guinness
      cake 121
berries: rustic cheesecake
      tower 56
   yogurt Bundt cake with
      fresh berries 90
   see also raspberries,
      strawberries etc
blackberry and apple cake
      132
blueberry and lemon drizzle
      cakes 33
bows 9
Brazil nuts: banana Brazil
      nut caramel cakes 85
brownie stack, naked 52
Bundt cake with fresh
      berries 90
bunting cake 60
buttercream 22, 44, 51, 117,
      124, 131, 135
   chocolate 106
   cinnamon 132
   hazelnut 136
   white chocolate 110

C

cake boards 9
candied carrots 94
candied hazelnuts 136
caramel: banana Brazil nut
      caramel cakes 85
   caramel icing 85
   caramel layer cake 43
   croquembouche 118
   praline 139
   spiced pear cake 82
carrots: candied carrots 94
   ginger cake with
      mascarpone and
      marigolds 127
   naked carrot cake squares
      94
Chantilly cream, strawberry
      layer cake with 18
charlottes: charlotte royale
      86
   lime charlotte cake 75
cheesecake tower 56
chequerboard cake 105
cherry and almond cakes
      with chocolate-dipped
      cherries 102
chestnut purée: chocolate
      chestnut cake 131
chocolate: chequerboard
      cake 105
   chocolate chestnut cake
      131
   chocolate-dipped cherries
      102
   chocolate fig cake 117
   chocolate Guinness cake
      121
   chocolate peppermint
      roulade 47
   ganache 89, 106, 131, 135
   icing 102
   naked brownie stack 52
   Neapolitan cakes 29
   orange and white
      chocolate dome cakes
      98
   passion fruit and
      chocolate layer cake
      106
   pretty bird cake 89
   pumpkin cake 135
   red velvet cake 30
   redcurrant cake 114
   rose and violet cake 71
   pear cake 82
   white chocolate
      buttercream 110
   white chocolate,
      peppermint and vanilla
      layer cake 110

choux pastry:
      croquembouche 118
Christmas cake, festive
      crumble 140
cinnamon buttercream
      132
clementine cakes 39
clotted cream: bunting cake
      60
   caramel layer cake 43
   crystallized flower garden
      cake 68
   macaron cake 67
coconut: coconut angel cake
      with raspberries 48
   icing 48
   naked carrot cake squares
      94
coffee: coffee and pineapple
      layer cake 113
   coffee and walnut cake
      139
Cointreau: festive crumble
      Christmas cake 140
colour, ombre effect sponge
      layers 8
cream: Chantilly cream 18
   ganache 89, 106, 131,
      135
   rose cream 21
cream cheese: frosting 17,
      30, 94
   lime charlotte cake 75
   rustic cheesecake tower
      56
crème patissière: redcurrant
      cake 114
croquembouche 118
crumble topping 140
crystallized flower garden
      cake 68
crystallized flowers 11, 26
custard cream: rhubarb and
      custard cake 128

D

decorations 8–9
dome cakes, orange and
      white chocolate 98
dowels 9
dried fruit: festive crumble
      Christmas cake 140

E

Earl Grey tea cake 63

F

festive crumble Christmas
      cake 140
figs: baked figs 117
   chocolate fig cake 117
flowers 9, 11
   crystallized 11, 26, 68
   flower garden timbale
      cakes 64
   ginger cake with
      mascarpone and
      marigolds 127
   lemon and lavender cakes
      124
   rose and violet cake 71
frosted mint leaves 47, 110
frosting: cream cheese
      frosting 17, 30, 94
   mascarpone frosting 121
   see also icing
fruit: rustic cheesecake
      tower 56
   yogurt Bundt cake with
      fresh berries 90
   see also raspberries,
      strawberries etc
fruit cakes: festive crumble
      Christmas cake 140

G

ganache 89, 106, 131, 135
ginger: ginger cake with
      mascarpone and
      marigolds 127
   gluten-free ginger and
      vanilla cake 97
glacé icing 139
glazes: caramel 43, 82
   salty honey 55
gluten-free ginger and
      vanilla cake 97
green tea ice cream cake
      109
Guinness cake, chocolate
      121

H

hazelnuts: buttercream 136
   candied hazelnuts 136
   hazelnut harvest cake 136
honey: Earl Grey tea cake 63
   salty honey cake 55
   spiced pear cake 82
honeycomb: Neapolitan
      cakes 29

I

ice cream: green tea ice
cream cake 109
icing: caramel 85
chocolate 102
coconut 48
glacé 139
lemon 33
see also glazes; frosting

J

jam/jelly: bunting cake 60
charlotte royale 86
chequerboard cake 105
crystallized flower garden
cake 68
macaron cake 67
mini Victoria layer cakes
76
orchard harvest sponge
cake 79

L

lavender: lemon and
lavender cakes 124
layering cakes 9
leaves, frosted mint 47, 110
lemon: blueberry and lemon
drizzle cakes 33
chocolate fig cake 117
icing 33
lemon and lavender cakes
124
lemon and raspberry
roulade 36
lemon meringue cake 40
summer flower ring cake
72
lime charlotte cake 75

M

macaron cake 67
Madeira wine: glazed
apricot cake 93
spiced pear cake 82
marigolds, ginger cake with
mascarpone and 127
marrons glacés: chocolate
chestnut cake 131
mascarpone cheese:
mascarpone cream 113,
127
mascarpone frosting 121
meringue: lemon meringue
cake 40
peach melba meringue
layer 25

mini Victoria layer cakes
76
miniature wedding cakes
22
mint: chocolate peppermint
roulade 47
frosted mint leaves 47, 110
white chocolate,
peppermint and vanilla
layer cake 110

N

naked Battenberg 51
naked brownie stack 52
naked carrot cake squares
94
naked fancies 44
Neapolitan cakes 29

O

oasis, flower 9
ombre effect sponge layers
8
oranges: clementine cakes
39
orange and white
chocolate dome cakes
98
orchard harvest sponge cake
79

P

passion fruit and chocolate
layer cake 106
peaches: orchard harvest
sponge cake 79
peach melba meringue
layer 25
pears: spiced pear cake 82
peppermint: chocolate
peppermint roulade 47
white chocolate,
peppermint and vanilla
layer cake 110
pineapple: coffee and
pineapple layer cake 113
pistachio layer cake 14
plums: orchard harvest
sponge cake 79
praline 139
pretty bird cake 89
profiteroles: croquembouche
118
pumpkin cake 135

Q

quantities 9

R

raspberries: coconut angel
cake with raspberries 48
lemon and raspberry
roulade 36
macaron cake 67
Neapolitan cakes 29
peach melba meringue
layer 25
red velvet cake 30
redcurrant cake 114
rhubarb and custard cake
128
ribbons 9
roses: crystallized rose petals
26
mini Victoria layer cakes
76
rose and violet cake 71
rose petal cake 26
Turkish delight cake 21
roulades: chocolate
peppermint roulade 47
lemon and raspberry
roulade 36
rum: festive crumble
Christmas cake 140
rustic cheesecake tower 56

S

salty honey cake 55
small cakes: banana Brazil
nut caramel cakes 85
blueberry and lemon
drizzle cakes 33
cherry and almond cakes
102
clementine cakes 39
flower garden timbale
cakes 64
lemon and lavender cakes
124
mini Victoria layer cakes
76
miniature wedding cakes
22
naked brownie stack 52
naked carrot cake squares
94
naked fancies 44
Neapolitan cakes 29
orange and white
chocolate dome cakes
98
redcurrant cake 114
spiced pear cake 82
sponge cake mixture 8

sponge finger biscuits/
ladyfinger cookies: lime
charlotte cake 75
spun sugar 118
stack, naked brownie 52
stencils 9
strawberries: charlotte
royale 86
lime charlotte cake 75
macaron cake 67
Neapolitan cakes 29
strawberry layer cake with
Chantilly cream 18
sugar, spun 118
sultanas/golden raisins: Earl
Grey tea cake 63
summer flower ring cake 72

T

tea: Earl Grey tea cake 63
green tea ice cream cake
109
tiered cakes 9
timbale cakes, flower garden
64
tuiles, rhubarb 128
Turkish delight cake 21

V

Valentine's layer cake 17
vanilla: gluten-free ginger
and vanilla cake 97
white chocolate,
peppermint and vanilla
layer cake 110
vanilla salt: salty honey cake
55
violets: rose and violet cake
71

W

walnuts: coffee and walnut
cake 139
wedding cakes: layering 9
miniature wedding cakes
22
white chocolate, peppermint
and vanilla layer cake
110

Y

yogurt Bundt cake with
fresh berries 90

Acknowledgments

Thank you to everyone at RPS for believing in this beautiful project – particular thanks to Cindy and Julia for commissioning the book, to Kate Eddison for all her patient editing, Leslie Harrington the Art Director and Lauren Wright for being an all-round star. Steve Painter and Lucy McKelvie, you did it yet again – this is my favourite-ever book due to your beautiful works of art and stunning photography. You worked magic with my recipes. Love to all at HHB agency for your continued support. To Gareth, Amy, Bowen and Hunter – although you are many miles away, you provide such amazing recipe inspiration – I love you guys. Thanks as well to my Mum and Mike and Dad and Liz for all their love and support while writing this book. With love and thanks to Kathy and Simon Brown, for all your edible flower inspiration. To all those who were kind enough to eat and critique all the cakes – Jane, Geoff, David, Lucy, Poppy, Jemima, Emma, Michael, Joy, Barry, the Bates family, Pauline, Miles, Jess, Josh, Rosie, Maren, Justina, Margaret, Pam, Tena and all at Amphenol, and a special mention of those members of WOAC who ate most of the cakes in this book – Russ, Charlotte, Dan, Stuart, Simon, Stuart, Tommy, Bob, Keith, Vernon, Katie, Little John, John, Chris, Deanna, Imogen, Amber, Oli, Pete, Pat and Eric – thank you all x